W9-ATQ-467

BUSINESS UNDER FIRE

BUSINESS UNDER FIRE

How Israeli Companies Are
Succeeding in the Face of Terror—
and What We Can Learn from Them

DAN CARRISON

NEW YORK • ATLANTA • BRUSSELS • CHICAGO • MEXICO CITY
SAN FRANCISCO • SHANGHAI • TOKYO • TORONTO • WASHINGTON, D.C.

Special discounts on bulk quantities of AMACOM books are available to corporations, professional associations, and other organizations. For details, contact Special Sales Department, AMACOM, a division of American Management Association, 1601 Broadway, New York, NY 10019.
Tel.: 212-903-8316. Fax: 212-903-8083.
Web site: www.amacombooks.org

Library of Congress Cataloging-in-Publication Data

Carrison, Dan.
Business under fire : how Israeli companies are succeeding in the face of terror—and what we can learn from them / Dan Carrison.
p. cm.
Includes index.
ISBN 0-8144-0839-7 (hardcover)
1. Israel—Economic conditions. 2. Corporations—Israel—Security measures. 3. Terrorism—Israel—Prevention. 4. Executives—Israel—Interviews. I. Title.

HC415.25.C37 2004
658.4'73—dc22

2004010295

Printing number

10 9 8 7 6 5 4 3 2 1

I wish to express my sincerest thanks to:

Yariv Ovadia, Consul for Communications and Public Affairs at the Consulate General of Israel in Los Angeles, and Doron Abrahami and Dara Rosenkranz of the Israeli Economic Mission, Los Angeles, without whose support this book would never have been possible.

Yoram Gilady, Rafi Brender, and Rona Kotler of the Israeli Ministry of Industry and Trade, whose cheerful support made my stay in Israel productive and wholly enjoyable. And Kobi Shemesh, who introduced me to the mysteries of Israeli traffic.

And, lastly, to Janos Damon, director of the Israeli Hotel Managers Association, who broke the ice for me with the hotel CEOs and general managers interviewed for this book.

Contents

■ ■ ■

. . . somewhere in the sands of the desert
A shape with lion body and the head of a man,
A gaze blank and pitiless as the sun,
Is moving its slow thighs, while all about it
Reel shadows of indignant desert birds. . . .
And what rough beast, its hour come round at last,
Slouches towards Bethlehem to be born?

—WILLIAM BUTLER YEATS, "THE SECOND COMING"

Author's Note

■ ■ ■

While researching the ways in which the Israeli business community has responded to an unrelenting campaign of terror, I immediately realized I would have to walk a fine line, lest I wander into territory well beyond the scope of the book—and certainly well beyond the experience of an American visitor. I made up my mind to focus solely on the management principles revealed to me, rather than on the crucible from which they have emerged. The Israeli-Palestinian conflict, therefore, is the context, not the content, of this business book. The origins and nuances of the terrorist crisis are subordinated by the business practices created to deal with it, just as the causes and characteristics of a hurricane are taken for granted in an emergency preparedness manual. It is my sincere hope—and, frankly, the hope of everyone I met in Israel—that this tragic conflict, which has caused so much suffering on both sides, will soon be resolved.

INTRODUCTION

Writing a Book on Business and Terror

■ ■ ■

"I love these journalists who visit Israel for three days, then go home and write the book Israel: Yesterday, Today, and Tomorrow."

—*YORAM ETTINGER, FORMER ISRAELI CONSUL GENERAL*

THE IDEA OF WRITING A BOOK ABOUT ISRAELI BUSINESS MANagement in the age of terror came to me one morning in front of the television set. I had just watched grim news media images of the aftermath of a suicide bombing. Having seen such images on the screen since the beginning of the *intifada,* in October 2000, I, like most Americans, had become somewhat inured to the horror of terrorist attacks against Israeli civilians. In this case, the target had been the passengers on yet another metropolitan bus. And, although the casualty toll had been high and particularly outrageous (the dead and wounded included many children), I found myself looking upon the scene from the perspective of a businessman. How, I wondered, do you run a bus company when your customers are being murdered in your buses?

Intuitively, I knew the answer couldn't be simply "increased security." How could any transportation company protect innumerable passengers from bombs, bullets, Molotov cocktails, and adjacent cars rigged with explosives, along hundreds of routes, over thousands of miles, for a single day, much less a year? I supposed that guards would be placed on buses, as a first step. But to what effect? And at what cost? And suppose the attacks simultaneously occurred, as they do in Israel, at restaurants, markets, coffee shops, and shopping malls? The wonder wasn't that Israelis still boarded buses to go to work; it was that there was still "work" to go to. Why weren't the businesses in Israel "out of business"?

As I drove to my office in the morning sun, I passed familiar and reassuring symbols of a vast status quo that I had taken for granted all of my life—the freeway itself, and the office buildings, factories, and retail stores along my route. I was part of the morning commute in Los Angeles; I was a member of what made the world turn round, the business community. And even though I had grumbled about my job the day before, I now counted myself lucky to travel in safety to an established company, with a huge customer base, in a strong economy. Whereas everyone in the world had a future, I was able to *plan* for mine. Life was stable in America and, for all practical purposes, predictable. Our economy, unlike that of Israel, was not under daily assault and had not been attacked since 9/11.

The more comfortable I felt, the more I pondered on what I imagined to be the opposite condition—business life in Israel. Then, by way of an unavoidable and possibly neurotic progression of thought, I imagined what it would be like *here* if random acts of terror were commonplace; if, for example, a sniper now waited patiently in the bushes by the road, or a suicide bomber melded in the line of passengers boarding the light rail bound for downtown. How would the American business community react to *years* of terror (four and counting, in Israel)? How would my company deal with managerial issues for which corporate policy has yet to be written? And how would I plan my business day, much less my career, in an economy under attack?

That's when I decided I would go to Israel. As a business writer, I felt I had a good chance of persuading somebody in the Israeli government to facilitate in-depth interviews with prominent business leaders, managers, and supervisors from a variety of industries. I wanted to learn how Israeli businesspeople coped with the terrorist crisis, and to see if their "best practices" would serve American companies well, even if—as we all hope—terror never strikes the United Sates with the punishing regularity experienced in Israel.

A few weeks later, I was granted an appointment with the Israeli Consulate in Los Angeles. I arrived with a package of credentials, including business books I had authored and coauthored. In a security vestibule, I emptied my pockets in front of a friendly but observant young man in a blazer. After passing through a metal detector, I was ushered into a hallway, where another young man greeted me and led me into his office. Yariv Ovadia, consul for communication and public affairs, presented a physical image I was soon to see frequently in Israel. Lean and alert, he had the look of a military officer, slightly incongruous in a civilian suit. Two other young people rose from chairs in his office. I shook hands with Doron Abrahami, consul for economic affairs, and Dara Rosenkranz, director of business development, both from the Israeli Economic Mission. Taking a seat, I suddenly felt as if I were in a job interview, under the scrutiny of three curious members of a younger generation, weaned on technology, speedy communications, and immediate results. Hoping my white hair lent a professorial air, I got to the point.

I told them I thought the American business community might have a lot to learn from Israeli CEOs and managers when it came to dealing with threats that, God forbid, may materialize in the United States. Just as our military and police have traveled to Israel to study under the experts, I wanted to go to Israel in order to interview business leaders who have been forced to become "experts" on leading their companies to success under the constant threat of terrorism. I showed them the books I had written; they were glanced at and left to lie on the table. I told them I had contacted a number of Israeli companies via e-mail, but that the responses had been slow in coming. I needed the help of the Israeli government, I said, to facilitate the interviews. Otherwise, it might be very difficult for an Irish-American to gain access to what I was beginning to perceive as an insular business community in order to explore a rather sensitive topic—the effect of terrorism on one's business.

The three young people before me listened politely, with unreadable faces. Doron had been taking occasional notes, or had perhaps been working on another problem, as he listened. Not sensing agreement from the other side of the table, I took a breath and started all over again.

Yariv held up and hand and nodded his head, as if to say listening to my spiel another time was unnecessary. He turned to Doron and asked with his eyebrows what his impression was. The room was silent; I was beginning to wonder if Israelis communicated telepathically. Doron held up the tablet he had been writing on. "Here," he said, "are the companies we can start with." Dara craned her neck to look at the list and suggested a few more. The blood began flowing back into my brain. I was going to get the assistance of the Israeli government!

Fingering a paper on his desk, Yariv asked me casually, "So, you are not afraid to go to Israel?"

And suddenly I was. The question, coming as it did from an authoritative source, nearly brought out an involuntary "Yes!" But I cleared my throat. "Of course not; I'm sure I'll be perfectly safe." The room was silent once more. I glanced out the window at the peaceful streets below. "Won't I?"

Yariv shrugged. "You have seen the news? There are suicide bombers."

"Well, yes, but surely. . . ." I was about to say something like, "Surely I'll be protected by a couple of guys in blue blazers and shoulder holsters."

Yariv was smiling now. "Dan, my grandmother lives there." His hand hovered about five feet over the carpet. "She is *this* tall, and in her seventies. Yet she goes to the market every day and rides the buses. She is not afraid. Israel is safer than Los Angeles. You will see."

When I walked out of the building I couldn't believe my luck. I was to have the advocacy of the Israeli government. Surely getting interviews with prominent Israeli business leaders should be a lot easier. Ideas had been tossed about the room by Yariv, Doron, and Dara—such as providing me with a driver from the Ministry of Industry and Trade to shuttle me to the interviews, and with a companion from the ministry to help with security and/or language issues. They noted that I'd need a hotel room, perhaps an El Al flight. I was very impressed by their hands-off attitude. They would help set up the interviews, but I could speak to whomever I wanted. All in all, a very productive meeting.

When I told my wife about the enthusiasm of the Israeli Consulate, it suddenly occurred to her that my pipe dream of traveling to Israel was about to materialize. Coincidentally, there had been a recent bombing in a Tel Aviv restaurant that killed twenty-one Israelis and wounded scores more. My wife, who rarely watches the news, had happened upon that story.

"You're not going," she said. "It's too dangerous over there."

And I understood, in a flash, why the Israeli tourism industry had been hit so hard.

A month or so later, my somewhat-reassured wife dropped me off at the El Al terminal at LAX. Having heard of the airline's security procedures, I was prepared for the third degree. I had asked for a letter of introduction from the Consulate's office, but of course, I left it on the dining room table in my haste to pack. A very pleasant young lady with a clipboard approached me. By now I was convinced that all Israelis in the public eye were in their middle twenties and that the older specimens were sequestered away, protected by their able children.

"And why are you traveling to Israel?" She had the frank, incorruptible look of a lady I once saw depicted on a Russian World War II propaganda poster. Mother Russia. Only this was Mother Israel. I told her I was writing a book on the Israeli economy, tactfully omitting the word *terror*. Turning on her heel, she said, "Come this way." I was led into a small room, where I watched my computer case and briefcase searched by hand. My bigger suitcase disappeared through an opening obscured by a curtain of rubber flaps. I was asked to leave my carry-on items in the room and to retrieve them once boarding had begun. I did so, two hours later, and was escorted with my briefcase and computer all the way to the boarding tunnel. No chance of somebody slipping a last-minute addition into my carry-on luggage.

After an eleven-hour flight, we arrived in Tel Aviv. My main contact in Israel would be Yoram Gilady, from the Ministry of Industry and Tourism. We had only communicated by e-mail, but he had the advantage of having seen my photo on a book jacket. As I walked into the terminal, I noticed a dark-haired man, maybe in his late forties, scowling in my direction. Looking about for the cheerful countenance of what I imagined a diplomat to have, I saw no likely candidate, only this rough-looking character at the end of the walkway. As I drew closer, he nodded his head, as if he had come to the conclusion that I was the right passenger. "You look older than your photo," he said, by way of a greeting.

I *felt* older, after the long flight. It occurred to me that Einstein had been mistaken: Youthful space travelers would not return to an aged earth; it was quite the reverse; I was living proof. As we walked out of the protection of the terminal into the open air of the parking lot, my fears of being in Israel returned. I became wary. This was, after all, a war zone. I glanced at the faces passing by, looking for signs of anxiety. I suppose I had imagined Israeli citizens furtively scurrying across the streets, avoiding the buses and coffee shops and living wary, joyless lives under the constant threat of terrorist attacks. I expected to see a society paralyzed by fear, and I steeled myself for the grim experience of interviewing business leaders who are trapped in an economy under siege.

The car from the Ministry of Industry and Trade pulled up. It was a little, light European car designed for little, light Europeans. My heart sank as I noticed that the rear windows were covered with funereal black curtains—no doubt to protect an important VIP, like myself, from assassination. As we drove off, I huddled in the shadows of the backseat. The driver, who had introduced himself as Kobi, saw me peeking through the curtains like the star witness in a Mafia trial, and he laughed out loud.

The curtains, he explained, were for the summer heat. "But this is winter," he said expansively, "so open za curtains." I did so, both literally and metaphorically, and what I saw during my time in Israel was a vibrant, resolute society with people packing the buses; cramming the coffee shops and nightclubs; and living lives of commitment, purpose, and hope.

CHAPTER ONE

The Assault on the Economy

■ ■ ■

"Very simply, the people stopped coming."

—*ARI MAROM, ISRAEL MINISTRY OF TOURISM*

THERE IS AN EXPRESSION USED BY ISRAELI BUSINESSPEOPLE, usually accompanied with a philosophic shrug, the way their forefathers might have shrugged off biblical events too big to do much about, like the Great Flood, the swarming locusts, drought, and pestilence.

DOUBLE PUNCH: NASDAQ AND NABLUS

"NASDAQ and Nablus" refers to a particularly cruel combination of events—the collapse of the high-tech bubble in the year 2000 and the nearly simultaneous beginning of the terrorist crisis still confronting the nation—both of which had a profound effect on the Israeli economy.

The crisis in the high-tech market would have been bad enough, especially since the Israeli economy was disproportionately invested in that sector. It must be remembered that Israel was considered a wasteland fifty years ago, without natural resources. Long thwarted by a boycott of Israeli products throughout the Middle East, the government made a big investment in its budding high-tech industry, hoping to garner a global market not subject to local tensions. With matching funds, it encouraged foreign investors to do likewise. By the year 2000, high-tech companies accounted for 25 percent of the gross domestic product (GDP), while products and services accounted for over 30 percent of Israeli exports. A hundred Israeli companies traded on Wall Street. The national economy was growing at a roaring 6.2 percent, while inflation was at a low of 1.3 percent. Foreign investment poured in, to the tune of $2 billion. But, as the NASDAQ suddenly plummeted in late 2000, and my 401(k) howled in protest, Israeli stock indexes fell at a rate of 37 percent.

Fortunately, the tourist industry was booming. While the techies were no doubt hoping the millennium would never come, as they worked overtime to meet the dreaded (and highly profitable) Y2K deadline, the hotels and restaurants couldn't wait for the twenty-first century to arrive. Religious groups the world over wished to meet the new millennium on the desert sands that had given birth to three major faiths. The hotels were booked solid, well into the new century. Hundreds of thousands of tourists, hoping to avoid the crowds, made reservations for later in the year. Every facet of the tourist industry prepared for the influx by investing in its infrastructure. By October 2000, tourism into Israel had broken all previous records; nearly three million visitors had spent their money inside the tiny nation.

Then, for reasons historians will debate for generations to come, the Palestinian *intifada* (Arabic for "shaking off") began in earnest by targeting Israeli civilians, including children, with successive waves of terror that continue at the time of this writing. Its effect on the tourist industry, and on the national economy as a whole, has been both crippling and, ironically, strengthening. Coming at the worst possible time, on the heels of the collapse of the high-tech bubble, this terrorist campaign has no historical parallel—in any part of the world.

HOW BAD IT'S BEEN

What is the best way to convey to the reader the magnitude of the terrorist problem? A list of the *hundreds* of attacks made against

Israeli civilians since the beginning of the intifada is not a particularly effective method of communication, because there is a tendency to speed-read through the accounts. Furthermore, a chronology of "successful" strikes against Israeli civilians would not tell the whole story; the vast majority of terrorist plans are foiled by Israeli security forces. Were it not for the vigilance of the police and military, the number of incidents would be absolutely staggering. The opposite approach would be to focus on one or two especially horrific atrocities, in which children have been shot in their beds and entire families murdered in a restaurant; but then the repetitive nature of the attacks is not sufficiently conveyed. And simply reporting the total number of murdered civilians makes an abstraction out of a recurring horror. Furthermore, the number is comparatively low from the perspective of an American living in a population of 280 million. But to an Israeli, living in a country of six million, a *thousand* indiscriminate murders is a national horror, especially in light of the fact that the crime of homicide has been almost unheard of in Israel.

Nor would the numbers of those killed convey the whole message. Those *injured* are often wounded for life—by nails first soaked in rat poison before being packed into an explosive belt. If a thousand unarmed civilians have been murdered, then thousands have been very seriously injured, which means that in this small country virtually everyone knows a victim of terror. Knowing a victim of terror, as opposed to *having known* a victim, almost precludes the healing process; it is a self-perpetuating trauma. The terrorists fully appreciate this effect and may be interested more in wounding than in killing. What spreads their message more effectively: scores of maimed citizens in the public eye—or the dead and buried? In a horrific spin on the adage "Out of sight, out of mind," the terrorists, by virtue of the weapons they have chosen (explosives packed with nails, bolts, and other forms of shrapnel), have decided the "walking wounded" are their best form of advertising.

The ripple effect of a terrorist attack is magnified inversely by a nation's size. The smaller the nation, the bigger the aftershock. This campaign against unarmed men, women, and children is being prosecuted in a country the size of New Jersey. It can be said without exaggeration that every Israeli knows someone who has been directly or indirectly affected by terrorism. The enormity of the situation does not appear to have been fully communicated to the rest of the world. We have all heard—and perhaps even expressed ourselves—comments such as "The cycle of violence in that part of the world has been going on for generations," as if by putting recent acts of terror in a historical context, we have dealt with the issue. But the only way to appreciate at least something of what Israelis are going through is to personalize these crimes in our own imaginations. We must imagine having our own loved ones outrageously torn out of existence. We must, in effect, "attend" the funerals of the victims of terrorism in order to feel the grief and outrage that has depleted the lives of so many Israelis.

And then, we must imagine what it would be like to run a business there.

Businesses do not operate in a vacuum; they are not floating abstractions, above the cares of life. There is, in fact, no clear distinction between everyday life and "business life." Those who enter the doors of the factory or a corporation cannot be expected to shuffle off the "mortal coil" and behave as if the terror in the street is a personal problem, to be suppressed during the workday. Every employee is the product of his off-premise environment. And Israeli managers, who are victims of the times themselves, must inspire and lead an often-traumatized workforce.

Interview with Amos Shapira, President, El Al Israel Airlines

"If you know how to exploit a crisis or a recession, then, when there is a recovery, you are in a better position."

Unsure of the battery life remaining in my tape recorder, I asked if we could stop at a store on the way to the interview. Kobi zipped into a parking place in front of a Staples office-supply house, which looked like any other Staples, except for the presence of a man with a gun on his hip and a metal detector at the front entrance. I glanced at the retail storefronts to my left and right—shoe stores, pharmacies, coffee shops—and each doorway was similarly guarded. Yoram, noticing my surprise, said cheerfully, "Well, at least a guard at every shop creates employment." His face then turned grave as he took in the scene of a city much changed from the days of his youth. "This is how we live, Dan."

At the airport main gate, we slowed to a stop alongside two young Israeli men in uniform, holding M16 rifles in a casual but ready stance. Yoram identified us, speaking in Hebrew, and I was given a suspicious look as we drove by, making me wonder if the guards thought I was a journalist. We met Amos Shapira, the president of El Al, one of the most highly regarded airlines in the world, in his office—a working-man's office, with papers and binders everywhere. In his midforties, he is the very personification of a "lean and mean" corporation, being lean and energetic himself. He is relatively new to the airline industry, coming from a career at Kimberly-Clark, where, he says with a self-deprecatory smile, he became an expert on diapers. In the Israeli Air Force he was a jet mechanic and today owns a private pilot's license. He took over the leadership at El Al smack in the middle of the intifada.

Q: You couldn't have picked a more challenging time to take control of El Al–right in the midst of the intifada, when passenger demand must have been plummeting. What was the first order of business?

Shapira: The first thing I did when I came aboard was to stabilize the schedules. Consistency and reliability is everything in this business. People depend on the schedules we set, and we cannot simply change them every day. Today, I am the only person authorized to cancel a flight because of commercial reasons [such as lack of passengers on the flight]. And usually [smiling], I'm hard to get.

On the other hand, it's very difficult to predict the demand that would in turn create a schedule. I heard a seminar the other day where someone said the fluctuation cycle in the airline industry is double the GDP cycle–and he was talking about the airline industry as a whole. The "future" in the airline industry is very hard to predict under the best of circumstances, much harder than in almost any other industry. But in Israel, it's worse yet; it's far more difficult to predict what will be the demand.

So, you try to make a forecast, and you make your schedule according to the forecast. Then reality comes, and demand is lower—let's say, by 10 percent. Ten percent can be disastrous in these days when the break-even load factor is very high. And that break-even point is much higher today—higher than 70 percent—due to increased security costs. This is the major challenge: to forecast demand, especially in this region, where demand can collapse in one quarter—such as in 2001, by 27 percent. A transatlantic flight from Tel Aviv to New York and back costs about a quarter of a million dollars. If you continue to fly with a very low-load factor, you can die within a month.

Q: So how do you handle a scheduled flight that, perhaps because of a bus bombing in Jerusalem, suddenly has 30 percent cancellations?

Shapira: Flexibility is very important—not in terms of schedules, because you want schedules to be consistent—but in terms of operations. For example, the fleet. Different planes, with different capacities, can be moved around to different routes in order to adjust to passenger demand. Or maybe I can take care of 80 percent of the demand with my fleet, and the other 20 percent with outsourced planes.

I came from Kimberly-Clark, where the market fluctuations were much less. We made diapers, and demand doesn't drop in that market. If we predicted a 5 percent growth and experienced only a 2 percent growth, we thought it was a disaster. In this airline industry, the unpredictable is predictable.

Q: That's an interesting point. How you present a business plan to your board of directors allows you to respond to the ever-changing political situation?

Shapira: You can *plan* for flexibility. For example, let's say I make a business plan for 2004. And I say to myself, "There, that's my plan." What I will do then is factor in a what-if scenario. For example, if I lease an aircraft, what kind of flexibility can I factor into the contract? This gives me room to respond to the crisis.

Somebody told me that comparing the management of a business today versus managing a business years ago is like comparing the old air-to-air missiles to modern ones. In the old days, when you saw the target, you fired and hoped it hit. If the target moved, you missed. With today's technology, the missile is constantly recalibrating, so if the target moves, it moves with it. It's the same with forecasting. You have to identify the target, then be able to change direction if the target moves.

Q: Security is such a touchy subject when it comes to marketing, because the very mention of the issue can frighten potential passengers. Does El Al try to reassure a nervous market that flying to Israel is safe?

Shapira: Why spend money on something that is well known? We have the best security systems in the world, and everybody knows it. That's because we spend two to three times more on security than any other airline in the world.

A good businessman should be optimistic by nature. If you run an airline, you should be crazy optimistic, because otherwise, how can you run such a business? I think the day will come when security will be less of an issue. So, if you spend all your marketing dollars to say, in effect, "Fly El Al because we have the best security," you will not resonate as much with the public when security is no longer the great issue it is today.

When I ask a passenger, "Why do you fly El Al?" and he tells me, "Because of your security," that's nice to hear, I suppose, but I'd much rather hear, "Because of your service."

Q: Have you ever flown with the flight crew, to show your support during a time of high tension?

Shapira: The only concerns I've ever had with the flight crew was during the SARS epidemic. We had a regular flight to Beijing—suspended for many months because nobody wanted to go there—and some of our people were concerned. So I flew with them. I'd never ask a crew to do something I wouldn't do.

Q: Did you ever second-guess your decision to leave Kimberly-Clark to run an operation subject to such swings in demand?

Shapira: Ah, but there is opportunity during a crisis! If you know how to exploit a crisis or a recession, then, when there is a recovery, you are in a better position. A crisis can sometimes be an opportunity for a company, because it gives you a window to become leaner and more efficient.

There is a saying: "When there is more jam, there are more flies." This market has shrunk; there are less competitors. When the competition returns, we will have stronger muscles; we'll be better able to compete.

Our financial results for [third quarter 2003] are actually better than in *better* years. We were at an 84 percent load factor.

Oddly enough, with terror strikes all over the world, many people see Israel as a safer place to visit because we've had so much experience in dealing with the problem.

■ ■ ■

PLANNING FOR FLEXIBILITY

I thought Shapira's concept of "flexibility" was delightfully offset by his stubborn reluctance to make *any* changes to the schedules his customers depend upon. It was refreshing to hear of flexibility as an aid to enforcing an ironclad agreement with the flying public, rather than as an arbitrary state of mind that could suddenly withdraw customer commitments, because those commitments now threaten the bottom line. His idea of flexibility was, in fact, a synthesis of modern-day crisis management and an old-fashioned determination to keep one's word.

It was noteworthy, too, that El Al's ability to respond to changing levels of customer demand was institutionalized beforehand (into the language of the airplane lease contract) by a methodical management philosophy; it is not a "ready-for-anything" attitude taken on in response to outside forces. No board of directors (BOD) would accept a business plan composed of possible responses to a list of scenarios—an "if that, then this" plan—because no firm steps would ever be taken towards the goals of the company, goals that may include changing the market's fickle behavior through one's determined adherence to the chartered course. Plans spell out actions to be taken, usually not in reaction to the market but because they are in the plan, regardless of the business environment. A hotel, for example, is somewhat like an airplane in that it depends on high occupancy to make a profit. But if a general manager commits to renovating the lobby, the work, once begun, continues despite downturns in the economy and despite poor occupancy. You might even argue the work continues *because* of poor occupancy, because the renovations are designed to attract more guests.

Shapira's "moving target" is customer demand, which is very difficult to forecast for any airline, especially one flying passengers to a country frequently in the news because its citizens are being mass murdered on buses and in restaurants. Since most news reports are followed by images of masked terrorists either celebrating or vowing continued attacks, the airline is subject to a nightmarish PR campaign not of its own making, as the media repeatedly broadcasts horrific street scenes with the promise of more to come. On the heels of this bad press comes the U.S. State Department's warning to Americans against traveling to Israel, and it is no wonder traditional tourist demand collapses with every attack. Not only does Shapira have to be "flexible"; he has to be, as he says, a "crazy optimist" just to remain in the business. And he has to hold to schedule as never before. What would the flying public's reaction be to canceled flights, if not a loss of confidence in the future of the airline? By having the ability to move with the target of customer demand through internal adjustments transparent to the customer (such as swapping planes with different capacities), Shapira is able to provide a sense of stability and chart a course for the future, despite the fluctuations of the market.

Coincidentally, the day after my interview with Amos Shapira, El Al posted its earnings for January through September 2003. The results were nothing short of spectacular. Revenues for the third quarter of 2003 were 39 percent higher than for the corresponding quarter of the previous year. Most dramatically, El Al's operating profit for the third quarter of 2003 was nearly $56 million, compared to a $26 million *loss* for the third quarter the previous year. Net profit for January through September 2003 more than doubled the previous year's performance: $12.4 million against $5.1 million the previous year. The third quarter of 2003, a year of crisis, was the best quarter El Al has had in ten years—not because the tourists were returning to Israel, but because Shapiro was credited for streamlining operations that saved the organization $10 million in the third quarter alone. Clearly, El Al had chosen, in the midst of the intifada, the right person to run the airline, even though Shapira came from an industry about as far as you can get from commercial airlines.

FINDING OPPORTUNITY IN A CRISIS

A crisis is a kind of Rorschach test in that one's responses reveal core personality traits. A "conservative" reaction to an organized terrorist assault on one's business might be to cease the very activities that created the business in the first place. Many of us would react to a threat by assuming a defensive posture; our very instincts might compel us to think first of protecting our assets, rather than exploring the uncharted waters of a market in turmoil. We become risk averse. Vowing not to be run off, we steel our will to endure the siege. Much rarer is the business leader whose immediate instinct is to attack the oncoming threat; rarer still is the leader who recognizes, and seizes, the opportunity to attack. I could not help thinking, as Amos Shapira spoke with a certain combative relish of exploiting the intifada, that he was such a leader. And I couldn't help smiling as I listened: Clearly the terrorists had rattled the wrong cage.

It is often cited that the Chinese symbol for "crisis" contains the character for "opportunity." The etymological roots for the English word is equally thought provoking, coming from the Greek word *krisis,* for "decision." Both are dynamic foundations, suggesting action and movement as opposed to the adoption of a rigid, fortress mentality. And, surely, there are many actions to be taken during a crisis that might otherwise have been more difficult. Temporary reductions in the workforce, pay cuts or freezes, the trimming of benefits—all will be accepted much more readily during a crisis, just as martial law is accepted by a populace during national emergencies. Permanent internal changes, as we shall learn in interviews to follow, sometimes occur to managers and owners in the midst of a crisis as a metaphorical palm heel on the forehead, as in, "Why didn't I think of this before?"

Shapira looks upon the intifada as a challenge that will make his company stronger, not weaker. Others interviewed for this book feel similarly. And this may be a bias more likely to be found with Israeli companies than elsewhere. Certainly, most business leaders shudder at the thought of an economic depression, no matter the cause. Throw in *terror* and it is all the more distressing because a remedy to the cause has yet to be found, which makes the duration of the consequence—the depression—unpredictable. One only has to watch the reaction on Wall Street to the slightest signal of turmoil within an industry, or an individual company, to see how much stomach the average stockholder has for unpredictability—and this is in a comparatively peaceful market. BODs and corporate executives feel the anxieties of the investor and watch apprehensively for further signs of market unrest. A number of the Israeli executives I interviewed had no doubt that their companies would emerge out of the current crisis for the better. That kind of mindset—no doubt an unintended consequence of the terrorists—is precisely what is needed to exploit that which other business leaders quite understandably fear.

What can those of us who are not experiencing a terrorist crisis learn from a business leader who not only sees a silver lining in the storm clouds above, but has found a way to extract the silver? Amos Shapira is not dealing with a terrorist crisis per se—*that* issue is relegated to the Israel Defense Forces (IDF). He is dealing with an economic depression, or more specifically, a depression manifested by a huge drop in incoming tourism. Tourists have turned away from countries for any number of reasons—the SARS epidemic, unfavorable currency exchange rates, revolution, oil spills, "red tide" algae infestations on the beaches, damage to the tourist infrastructure due to a massive hurricane, etc. The strategies developed by Shapira for this particular crisis—providing customer consistency in a truly volatile environment, implementing flexibility to counter imperfect forecasting, introducing cost-effective marketing, and not allowing a corporate strength (in this case, airline security) to become a raison d'être—would, no doubt, serve any company, despite the origin of the crisis it finds itself confronting.

■ ■ ■

Interview with Ari Marom, Director, North American Operations, Israel Ministry of Tourism

"The ripple effect throughout the national economy has been widespread."

As Yoram and I headed for the Ministry of Tourism, I marveled at the way Israelis drive. If there was danger in Israel, this was it. Drivers zipped in and out of lanes with perfect abandon. Those not content with the suicidal speeds would tailgate the car in front, within inches, before passing. I looked over Kobi's shoulder at the speedometer; the high values of the kilometer scale only added to the sense of speed as he competed with his fellow citizens in what seemed to be a life-and-death race to work. To position himself to pass another car, Kobi had an interesting way of straddling the middle hash marks on the road so that we occupied two lanes simultaneously for miles. Time and again, I could see what impossible maneuver he was about to attempt and prayed that he would come to his senses. Cinching my seat belt ever tighter, and mentally practicing rolling into a ball, I marveled at Yoram's equanimity as he relaxed, smoking a cigarette, in the front passenger seat, inches away from sudden death. Yoram is pretty solid, at maybe 180 pounds. Glad to have such a substantial human airbag in front of me, I asked, against the rushing wind, what he knew about our upcoming interviewee, Ari Marom.

"He's been with the Ministry of Tourism for years," Yoram hollered back. "Now he's the director of North American Operations. He can tell you what has happened to our tourist industry."

Ari Marom is a trim, nice-looking guy in his midforties. He immigrated to Israel from Canada as a young man and served as a paratrooper in the IDF. Like all able-bodied Israeli males, he spent another twenty years in the active reserve. When I asked him how many jumps he had had, he answered, with a ready laugh, "One is too many."

Q: How badly has the tourist industry been hit by the intifada?

Marom: Let me start from the beginning. The year 2000—the millennium—was a peak year for us. Nearly two and a half million tourists came to Israel. Based on reservations, we expected to have even more the following year, because a lot of people thought it would be just too crazy here during the millennium. Tourist revenues in 2000 added up to 4.3 billion U.S. dollars. Then, in October of that year, the terror attacks began. The following year, instead of the huge influx of tourists we had expected, and even built for, about 850,000 came. The year after that it was worse. We lost a billion dollars of expected revenue while costs, such as security, went way up. Cities like Jerusalem, or Tiberius, which have no industry to speak of, other than the tourist industry, were hit the hardest.

Q: I remember hearing ads for Israeli tourism on Los Angeles radio stations that always ended with the refrain, "Nobody belongs in Israel more than you." Then, a couple of years ago, the ads stopped. I never heard another.

Marom: Yes, that was our campaign. We stopped it because there was no point in mass advertising. The people from abroad were not going to come. Our approach now is very focused on markets that we *know* are coming here in spite of the situation and, in some case, because of the situation—like the Christian evangelicals and the Jewish community in America. Both want to support us. There has even been created in the States the concept of virtual tourists—that is, people coming, carrying the money of those who were unable to come, but who wanted their dollars spent in Israel.

We are also focused on domestic tourism, much more so than in the past. As a consequence, many of our hotels are full on Saturday nights with Israelis. The problem is, they're empty again for the rest of the week. Not empty, but at, say, 20 to 30 percent occupancy.

Q: The news media can do much more damage to an economy than a suicide bomber—not because they report on the bombing, but because they report on nothing else. Is there any way the Ministry of Tourism, or the hotels collectively, can counter the media?

Marom: [Nodding his head] The media is tricky. You have to remember, we need the media to get our message out. A good part of our marketing activities are through hosting journalists. But we also know how much damage the media can do to us when it feeds on graphic, sensationalist images. We can't create an alternate media. We have to use the media when it's to our advantage. I don't think they're out to get us. It's just that bad news sells better than good news.

I can tell you, though, the Israeli government finally grew tired of CNN's reporting and threatened to cut them off in Israel. A lot of CNN executives flew out here to save the market.

But one way to counter the media messages of doom and gloom is through word of mouth. Word of mouth is more important in the tourist industry than maybe in any other. Think about it: This is the only form of business in which you are halfway around the world, paying somebody an awful lot of money for something you're not going to see in six months. If you get to the hotel and it's a dump, or the service is terrible, it's too bad; they've got your money. So before you go, you check around. And, which are you going to believe: a commercial from the hotel, or the personal experience of a friend who has actually been there?

Q: I remember reading that in Egypt a few years ago, there were machine-gun attacks against tourist buses heading for the pyramids. Have attacks like that happened here?

Marom: No. There have been almost no direct attacks upon the actual tourists themselves, despite countless opportunities. The Muslim and Arab population, by and large, also makes their living from tourism. I suppose the terrorists know better than to bite the hand that feeds them.

Q: That's ironic, isn't it? The tourists themselves have been spared direct attacks, and thank God. But the Israeli tourist industry, as a whole, has been nearly mortally wounded. Was that their intended target all along?

Marom: Not just the tourist industry. The ripple effect throughout the national economy has been widespread. What business, in the long run, is *not* affected by the sudden and massive reduction of incoming visitors with money to spend?

▪ ▪ ▪

THE IMPORTANCE OF WORD-OF-MOUTH ADVERTISING

When confronted with the awesome power of news images, a word-of-mouth campaign seems inadequate indeed. For one thing, the numbers of potential tourists whose opinions can be influenced by a personal recommendation are minuscule, compared to the vast international audience exposed to grim reports of a country in turmoil. Secondly, it could not be a "campaign" at all. Even ecstatic returning tourists do not normally rush about telling the world about their wonderful vacation in Israel; that story is much more likely volunteered when advice is sought. So, how could even the most ebullient word-of-mouth "advertising" possibly counter repetitive news broadcasts that, in so many words, warn the civilized world not to vacation in Israel?

The answer can be seen by reversing the values for a moment—that is, by considering the damage *negative* word-of-mouth messages can wreak. A movie star, for example, with a very powerful public relations apparatus at her disposal, may not be able to dispel a certain rumor, even though that rumor is never published or broadcast and is spread simply by word of mouth, by average folks who do not know, and have no hope of ever meeting, the celebrity. "Whisper campaigns" are often employed in political races, the efficacies of which can be attested to by many a defeated candidate.

Conspiracies, scandalous liaisons, behind-the-scenes manipulations of powerful ethnicities, alien bodies kept at a top-secret air force base—these and scores of other "secrets" become the sure and certain knowledge of armies of believers who heard it through the grapevine. Clearly, word-of-mouth campaigns can be very effective, for better or for worse, even in the face of well-publicized denials broadcast by powerful media outlets.

We have all waited in lines at restaurants that do not advertise, their reputations having been built by those in the know. Car manufacturers have been occasionally surprised by widespread demand for a model that has not been heavily advertised. Insurgent candidates, without the political machinery of the incumbent, have often been gratified by grassroots movements, spread solely by word of mouth. The business that wishes to facilitate the process beyond the "tell your friends" stage would do well to set up a community on its Web site, making it easy for all forum participants (existing and potential customers, industry professionals, etc.) to swap information and stories about virtually anything. Frank testimonials and friendly advice will be passed along, often countering public misconceptions. Ari Marom's rhetorical question, "Who are you going to believe: a friend who has actually stayed at the hotel you are considering, or a commercial for the hotel?" can be applied to the terrorist crisis. Who are you going to believe: a friend who has vacationed in Israel, or the news media?

REDEFINING THE MARKET

Many American readers will be familiar with a highly successful and very clever ad campaign for the online travel agency Expedia. Its commercials are variations on the following scenario: A couple searches the Internet, planning a vacation. An apparent paradise is found, but the daydreamers are suddenly assaulted with visions of a vacation gone bad due to haphazard associations with the prospective destination (mosquitoes, insurmountable language problems, etc.). The humorous point of the ad campaign is that the solution—another, much more relaxing destination—is only a click of the mouse away. There would be no humor in a parody of this commercial, in which the prospective vacationers select Israel as the ideal vacation spot and are then assailed by fantasies of bus bombings and fanatic terrorists attacking their restaurant as they dine. But the Ministry of Tourism knew very well that these were exactly the kinds of images people have come to associate with Israel. It wasn't an accurate impression, with regard to tourists, but no amount of expensive advertising could overcome it. Suddenly, "No one belongs in Israel more than you" seemed, in light of the violence, very dark humor indeed.

It is not easy for any organization—a government agency or a corporation—to abandon a heretofore extremely profitable marketing campaign, especially when it knows the target groups are still out there and still in need of what it offers. The frustration alone would tempt any true believer in a product to try once again, perhaps in a variation of the message, to reach the once-friendly audience. It is very difficult to admit to oneself that a successful campaign must be suspended, for no other reason than a global misconception is stronger than the most earnest attempts to educate the customer. Although not expressed by Ari Marom, there must also have been a sense of undeserved rejection on the part of his marketing staff, not to mention his countrymen; and that creates a managerial challenge in itself. Through no fault of their own, the plan must be abandoned and replaced with new strategies for markets that have been traditionally dismissed as not particularly fertile. No longer encouraged to "think big," the marketing departments must think in terms of survival and try to replace the single-sourced big numbers with scattered contributions from here and there.

The ministry's venture into new marketing territory mimicked those of the hotels. By focusing on domestic tourism, local business groups, and the Jewish and Christian communities in the United States, the Israeli tourist industry has been able to stop the bleeding. At the time of this writing, the once-crowded hotels in Jerusalem and Tel Aviv are averaging 25 percent to 30 percent occupancy; many of them are even making a *profit,* thanks to measures taken that will interest managers from any industry. Much of this business, attracted by new marketing campaigns, is new to the hotels.

When the crisis passes and the tourists return, these hotels will enjoy heretofore unknown levels of activity. The traditional tourist base will be bolstered by yet another 25 percent that never really existed before the industry adapted to the changes wrought by the terrorists.

■ ■ ■

Interview with Chen Michaeli, General Manager, Dan Panorama Hotel

"The owners were seriously thinking of closing down the hotels."

Chen Michaeli is in his early forties and athletic. He has a face that was made to smile. Cheerful and debonair, he was born to be a general manager of a luxurious hotel. And the Dan Panorama in Jerusalem is certainly that. The lobby—walls, floor, and ceiling—is completely lined with glistening marble. With the works of art on display, I had the impression of being inside a museum or palace. It hardly seemed possible that outside the sanctuary of this elegant hotel there had ever been a problem with terrorism. Chen led me into a conference room and slapped down a printed PowerPoint presentation on the mahogany table.

Michaeli: That, my friend, is a lecture I gave to the members of the Israeli Hotel Managers Association late in 2001. The intifada had been going on for a year. We were at our lowest occupancy ever–with the exception of January and February of 2003 [before the start of the Iraq War]. This talk was about the choice of closing down the hotels or finding a way to keep them open.

Q: That must have been a sobering meeting.

Michaeli: Oh yes, it was very serious, indeed. Hotel managers from all over the country were there, each of them facing the greatest challenge of their careers.

The owners were seriously thinking of closing down the hotels. They had experienced the intifada for a year and they could not continue to lose money at 15 percent occupancy. What *we* had to do, as the general managers, was to show the owners there were alternatives. We had to prepare a business case, showing them how much it would cost to shut the doors, and how much to stay open, even at these terrible occupancies. For example, closing down the Dan Panorama would have cost $60,000 a month. As long as we can lose less than that, we might as well stay open.

Q: Why would the recurring costs be so high, if the hotel were shut down?

Michaeli: Because one day it will reopen again; you don't just lock the door and walk away. Look at some of the costs involved: severance for the employees, maintenance of hotel and grounds, security, energy bills, property and third-party insurance, taxes—which are very high in Israel, by the way, nearly $25,000 monthly—management fees, telephone fixed costs, previous advertising commitments, reopening costs, recruiting and training of new employees. And this is not to mention the subjective costs—such as damage to image, loss of loyal guests, and losing good employees—some of which are the reasons guests return.

Q: So, having established the costs for closing, you still had to find a way to make enough money to offset those costs. How does a hotel make a profit at 15 percent occupancy?

Michaeli: Well, the next step was to reengineer the hotel, to see what it would cost to remain open *as a hotel designed to meet this crisis.*

So I had to take a step back and look at the hotel critically. The fact that we have 300 rooms is only relevant on a Friday night, when we do have a fair amount of Israeli guests for the weekend. But with low occupancies from Saturday afternoon through the rest of the week until Friday night, we only need a hundred rooms. So, let's restructure the hotel as if it were a 100-room hotel and construct the organizational chart accordingly.

I asked, "What would it take to run a hundred-room hotel?" Then, once we got the model, I told my managers, "Using this model, go run a 300-room hotel." Since then, we've managed to maintain an organizational chart for a hundred-room hotel while running a 300-room hotel.

Q: I imagine a lot of people had to be let go. How did you motivate those who remained?

Michaeli: We told the surviving employees, "We are set. We have designed the hotel for the worst, and there will be no more firings. However, there will also be no more raises, training, and employee outings." It was important that everyone knew what we were going to do, and what we were *not* going to do, so they wouldn't be disappointed by false expectations.

The effect was dramatic. Suddenly each employee felt that he or she was more important to the organization than before. They have a broader picture of their job, the organization, and how to contribute to it.

Q: What was the effect of the reengineering on you? I mean, general managers of luxury hotels are a pretty suave lot.

Michaeli: [Grinning] Yes, it's a bit rough on the ego. Hotel managers have gotten used to divisions, and departments, and assistants, and a staff that responds to a snap of the fingers. Let's face it, this can be a glamorous business. You deal with people from all over the world. There are big meetings and symbols of power; it's a great life. But now, since the intifada, a manager may find himself doing tasks that years ago he would have thought beneath him, such as checking rooms, supervising housekeepers, you name it.

Q: With the downsizing in staff, have the guests noticed a decline in amenities?

Michaeli: You know, it's almost the opposite. While the variety of services went down—less dining rooms, for example—the quality of personal service went up. The flatter the pyramid, the more direct contact between managers and guests is possible, and between the employees and guests.

Q: Would you say that Jerusalem has been the hardest hit?

Michaeli: Yes, Jerusalem and Tiberius, and that's because we are totally dependent upon tourism. But in some ways we are better off than Tel Aviv. Orthodox Jews come here for the weekends, and there is some tourism from the evangelical Christians, who want to see the holy sites. The [U.S.] State Department has advised against traveling to Israel, meaning corporate accounts from abroad are discouraged, and that hurts the hotels in Tel Aviv more than in Jerusalem.

Another thing has helped us, and that is a program started by two Israeli businessmen in response to the intifada. It's called Birthright Israel. A fund has been created to subsidize a trip to Israel for virtually every Jewish boy or girl at the age of eighteen who has never been. Other Jewish agencies and donors and the Israeli government also contributed. For the last three years 5,000 to10,000 [young adults] come to the country for a ten-day visit. Trip, hotel, meals all free.

Normally a hotel like ours wouldn't dream of participating, because I don't have to tell you what it is like to host 200 eighteen-year-olds from the States coming here for a holiday. But, during this crisis, it was a welcome piece of business.

Q: You're in a business where you have to smile. What is it like here, after a terrorist attack? How do you reassure the guests?

Michaeli: Not just the guests, I have to reassure the employees, most of whom are Israeli Arabs. After a suicide bombing, they come to work looking pretty miserable. But they, too, must smile for the guests, so we in management must assure them that we understand, and that it's okay, and that they are trusted members of the family.

As to the guests, we've had bombings close enough to be *heard* by those in the hotel. Most of our guests, however, are with groups and they knew there might be an attack. They take it very bravely, I must say. The next day, they're back on track.

Q: Let's talk for a moment about planning. I imagine it's pretty hard to predict demand, given the decline in tourism. Nevertheless, your owners are looking to you for a business plan, beyond the one that convinced them to stay open. How do you prepare that, and are they satisfied with grim projections?

Michaeli: Well, first of all a "tourist" may not really be a "tourist" as far as the hotel business is concerned. For example, a family can come here and stay with the mother-in-law. But, yes, we have to predict demand and plan accordingly.

We realized the difficulty of planning, early in the crisis. Usually, you use the current year as the basis for the following year. This is how we might have planned for 2001. The benchmark *then*, however, was a record year, the best ever. Ironically, the intifada started in October of 2000, just as we were beginning to prepare the budget. The best we could do was come up with a six-month plan. We predicted abysmal figures for the first six months of 2001 and we, unfortunately, were right. We *did* hope for a change for the better, because in the past things generally got better after a few months of unrest. But by July [2001], it was clear to everybody that this was different, and that it could last years. So the industry prepared for a long haul. Then came the 9/11 attacks in the United States, when people stopped flying, and the Iraqi War in 2003—and things got even worse.

We are very realistic in our projections. And the owner understands that, with the decline in tourism, even if we were to become the most successful hotel in Jerusalem, it would still mean only 30 to 40 percent occupancy per month.

Q: You were in the military?

Michaeli: [With a mock salute] Yes, antiaircraft officer.

Q: Did that training help you plan for the unexpected?

Michaeli: Obligatory military service is a two-edged sword. You can achieve less because of those three years. Somebody else, in another country without compulsory service, gets a three-year career head start. *But,* we learn how to improvise. Most Israelis will do zero planning and 100 percent improvising. We go a little too far in that direction, I'll admit, but it's a talent learned in the military.

Q: What has been the greatest lesson for you, during this crisis?

Michaeli: How little we knew about the hotel business before the intifada. Years ago we thought we were the most efficient, cleverest managers in the industry. Every year we thought nothing else could be done to improve our efficiency. Then the intifada came along and opened our eyes to revolutionary possibilities we never saw before. We definitely weren't as smart as we thought we were back then.

■ ■ ■

TAKING IT TO THE OWNERS

One would think that general managers of major hotels have close working relationships with their owners, just as luxury liner captains must with the owners of the shipping line. And, like captains, the GMs must be given a pretty free hand in running their hotels; otherwise the on-the-spot decision making would be a cumbersome process, especially if the owners reside out of country. Nevertheless, it's a safe bet that certain decisions from on high—regarding hotel "chain" policy, stock splits, or the purchase of new hotels—are occasionally handed down to the general managers without solicitation of their input. Chen Michaeli and his fellow GMs in the Israeli Hotel Managers Association had every right to anticipate the possibility of their respective hotels being shut down; some, in fact, had already been closed. The prestigious Hyatt chain had pulled out of Jerusalem after several terrorist attacks, including the assassination of the minister of tourism in its hotel. The likelihood of more troubled owners and investors simply closing down shop in Jerusalem—arguably the Israeli city hit hardest by the intifada—was high enough for GMs like Michaeli to take the lead in developing a business case for keeping the hotels open.

The meeting of the Israeli Hotel Managers Association, in which Chen Michaeli shared the business case he was about to take to his owner, must rank with the most serious business meetings of all time. Every manager in that room faced the greatest challenge of his career. Those who loved the hotel industry, and therefore wanted to remain in it, knew they were in for the fight of their lives—not the least of which would be persuading their owners to keep the doors open. Everyone knew that 20 percent occupancy for even a few months meant bankruptcy. The tourists had stopped coming, and there was every indication they would not return in the near future, and perhaps for years to come. You could not have blamed the most sympathetic, even the most patriotic, hotel owner for cutting the losses, sooner rather than later. It is noteworthy, I think, that Israeli hotel managers, and the people they supervised, did not wait around for the axe to fall.

Anyone who has ever been through a merger, or the sell-off of a subsidiary, or the closing down of a production facility knows the feeling of helplessness shared by all within the organization who must wait while the "powers that be" make the fatal decision. The suggestion that these remote decision makers might be open to persuasion is often met with derision. There is a sense among the employees that the owners and investors can be moved only by financial considerations and that, furthermore, *because* they are owners and investors, they already know the numbers do not pencil out.

It seems, however, that Michaeli and his associates did not take it for granted that the owners, and the owner's accountants, had all the pertinent information, so they took it upon themselves to make sure every relevant aspect of each case was considered. It makes perfect sense that those closest to the task take on this responsibility. The owners, for all their savvy, may not see the possibilities those "in the trenches" are motivated to discover, or to create. Furthermore, the owners *want* to hear sound reasons why their investments are still viable. The business case prepared by Chen Michaeli came as a kind of revelation—if we are to go by his statement that, before the intifada, Israeli hotel managers *already* thought they were the best in the world. Creative operational responses to backbreaking, low occupancies came out of the process of preparing the argument for keeping the Dan Panorama, and hotels like it, open for business. Had the managers simply waited for the owners and investors—many of whom live in Europe—to decide whether to close the hotels, it is likely that a number of them would have been shut down. Instead, these hotels are in the process of revolutionizing the entire industry, worldwide.

■ ■ ■

Interview with Eyal Kaplan, General Partner, Walden Israel Venture Capital

"I point out to them that, of all of our portfolio companies, the only one that has been directly hit by terrorists was a subsidiary located in the World Trade Center. And I ask them, 'Would you stop investing in New York?'"

Tourists were not the only people who stopped coming to Israel; investors, too, feared for their personal safety, and for the safety of their investments. My next interview was with Eyal Kaplan, general partner of Walden Israel, a highly regarded venture capital firm near Tel Aviv. Eyal Kaplan is in his midforties, trim, with thick, prematurely gray hair. He had just flown home from New York and was fighting a raspy throat.

Kaplan: Walden is a venture capital firm; we raise money from institutional investors, mainly from Europe and the United States. We started to raise our most current fund four days after the intifada began. It was an uphill battle. We flew around trying to raise money. If it was an hour meeting, we found ourselves answering questions for the first forty-five minutes about the geopolitical situation, stability, and political risk, instead of the investment opportunities, our track record, etc. It was a real challenge. Those who had invested with us before, and who had visited Israel before, were still for the most part open to investment. The first-timers, however, were a lost cause.

Q: Can't familiarity with Israel be a double-edged sword? Those who know Israel also know there has never been an intifada that has lasted years. Did you have to explain why this period of terror is starting its fourth year, and try to predict when it will end?

Kaplan: Those familiar with the Israeli environment knew that we've battled terrorism for decades; nonetheless, the return on the investment dollar has been very satisfying, so maybe they think this is what makes our companies stronger. People who have never been here learn all they know about Israel from CNN and the BBC. They are not going to invest.

Q: Did your investors typically visit Israel before this current crisis?

Kaplan: Investors normally like to visit the country first; they want to kick the tires before they make an important investment decision. Before the intifada, everyone would come. Once the terror attacks began, the first-timers would not come. They invested in other countries.

Those who had been here before didn't want to come either, but at least they were open to investing. They still wanted to kick the tires, so they asked the companies in our portfolio to come to them instead. So that's what happened.

There is what we call here "the spouse effect." The vast majority of our contacts who do not come refrain because of the spouse or the families. Let's face it, they are concerned. Besides, most corporate travel insurance policies do not cover people when the U.S. State Department issues a travel advisory. I've had investors tell me, "I'd like to come, but we can't get insurance."

We eliminate some of the hesitation by saying, in effect, "Okay, Israel, as dangerous as it might be, is a great place to invest. We're here; you don't have to be here. We'll do the job for you because we're here on the ground." This way, we take away the psychological effect of personal risk. So now the question rises to a more institutional level. Our investors ask: "Do we want our *money* to be at risk in this geopolitical environment?"

Q: Sure, there are so many other places in the world to invest in that are not troubled by unrest. Is Israel a hard sell?

Kaplan: Well, I point out to them that, of all of our portfolio companies, the only one that has been directly hit by terrorists was a subsidiary located in the World Trade Center. And I ask them, "Would you stop investing in New York?"

Then, to calm their fears, the companies we represent will share their contingency plans with the investors so that they're confident we can recover.

But really, this business of venture capital is based primarily on relationships and trust, rather than specific opportunities. In our situation we have five anchor investors—four from the U.S. and one from Europe—and then a group of smaller investors. These people essentially give us their money to use for ten years—and pray. The money is in our hands, and they trust our discretion because of our track record. So our relationships are quite strong. In fact, after a well-publicized terror attack, we get phone calls alright, but not because they are concerned about their investments; they want to know if we're alright and if our families are alright.

I get the feeling our investors admire us. There is a very high degree of appreciation for us, who are willing to live in this country and who wake up and go to work every day and continue to demonstrate that we're doing all we can to make their investment work. So, rather than put pressure on us, they go out of their way to support us.

Our investors look at us and think: "These guys deliver. I don't know exactly how they do it. If it was me living in Israel I might be paralyzed in my home—or obsessed with the safety and whereabouts of my family—but somehow they come to the office and deliver the results. Go figure."

Q: Do you think that's how the business communities in other countries might react to terror?

Kaplan: I'm not sure. I do know that Israelis handle crises very well. Look at the collapse of the dot-com industry. In Silicon Valley and in Europe, thousands of companies shut down at the first sign of trouble. Israeli companies fared much better. They immediately scrambled for more new markets and went to Japan, and to Germany.

You have to remember, we're used to this. I remember the Six Day War when I was seven, and the Yom Kippur War when I was fourteen. I guess I'm a product of my childhood. Maybe if I had grown up in Australia I'd have a different personality.

Like every Israeli, I was in the military. People have tried to kill me.

Am I going to shake in my boots simply because a customer no longer wants to buy my merchandise?

Q: What did you do in the military?

Kaplan: I was a paratrooper, and then [making a dismissive gesture of the hand] some other things.

Q: As you say, every Israeli has served in the military. Does that help them in business?

Kaplan: Yes, in a couple of ways. For one, we are very focused and very realistic here, and that comes from military training. Israeli companies here are not spinning grandiose business schemes; they are focused on solving immediate problems. Maybe Israelis are not so good at creating $10 billion companies in two years which take over the world, but if you need a team of software or hardware engineers to solve a problem better than anyone else—without ever giving up—faster and cheaper than anyone else, you can't do better than Israelis. That's why our small start-up companies are so successful; and they [are] very often begun by former military buddies.

Secondly, maybe military training makes us defiant. We have to prove to the world that they made a mistake when they didn't invest in Israel because of the terrorist situation. And every businessperson I know feels the same way. We are driven to show the world how good we are, especially during times of crises.

Q: How does living here affect family life?

Kaplan: In the Maxima restaurant bombing in Haifa, twenty-one were killed, and I think sixty-four wounded. The little boy who sat next to my daughter in school was killed. His parents and grandparents were very badly wounded. In a previous attack, another child was killed from the same school.

During the Gulf War and the Iraq War, our children went to school with a gas mask in one hand and a lunch box in the other. My daughter had a birthday at school; all the children came, each with a gas mask on their shoulder. My American friends are more freaked by this than they are by reports of suicide bombers.

But, at the end of the day, you have to weigh the whole thing. I'll ask you a question: Do you let your child walk to school in L.A.? Would you want your wife to park at the end of the mall parking lot at night, then walk to the store? Probably not. But those are not problems here. So what happens more often—your kid walking to school, or a bus exploding?

Q: I can't imagine watching my kids go to school with a gas mask in hand. Have you ever thought of leaving Israel, if only for the sake of your family?

Kaplan: No. Here, we are all in this together. In Israel, we are a group-oriented culture. It might be hard for you to appreciate what it's like here, because in America it's difficult to keep childhood friends. Here, we all grow up together. The same circle of friends just keeps on expanding rather than changing.

America is the culture of the individual. The individual takes full responsibility for himself or herself, and the individual goes out and takes on the world. Here, it's the group, or the tribe, which takes full responsibility for itself and takes on the world together.

I'll give you an example. My wife, who is from America, always laughs after we return from a parent-teacher conference. First, the teacher praises our daughter for being so well liked. Then she praises [her] for the friends she has. Then, during the last two minutes of the conference, the teacher adds, as an afterthought: "Oh, and by the way, her grades are very good."

■ ■ ■

THE IMPORTANCE OF SHARING A CONTINGENCY PLAN

There are any number of reasons why a manager may not initially wish to bring up the subject of contingency plans to an important customer or investor. Most of us have, at some time or other, volunteered information to a customer that unwittingly led to a chain of other questions we would have preferred not to field. Just as old salts in the military advise the young recruit to "never volunteer," sales managers caution their sales force not to oversell, and not to bring up ancillary information unless the customer specifically asks for it. Many a contract has been lost because the customer suddenly wanted to "think about" new information, suddenly introduced. Certainly, the subject of a contingency plan, if broached, can evoke images in the customer's mind that do not contribute to a warm, fuzzy feeling about the pending transaction. What, after all, is the contingency plan designed to counter? *A terrorist attack!* A customer or investor might recoil from the prospect of placing his investment in a business threatened by sabotage.

In addition to not wanting to bring up a controversial subject, the manager may not want the competition to be aware of his backup plan; after all, customers do talk to the competition. A manager may not want to discuss the issue, for fear of sending an ambiguous signal to his workforce, which should under no circumstances feel as if there is an alternative to the marching orders already given. And, finally, a manager may not even *have* a backup plan, mainly because he feels there is not sufficient danger to warrant the investment of time, money, and energy to create emergency alternatives that will never be used. If the truth were to be known, many Israeli businesspeople do not think a contingency plan necessary; the nation's defense forces provide for a safe business environment, thank you very much. There are exceptions—bus companies, for one—but, generally speaking, the Israeli business infrastructure is rather unaffected by terrorism. Factories and software houses continue to deliver on time. Why add credence to a problem that exists only in the customer's imagination?

The possibility of an Israeli business failing to meet its contractual obligations, although remote in reality, may, however, seem very likely to a customer from abroad weaned on grim news reports. And if the company in question is a sole-source provider, the customer may be tempted to develop a contingency plan of his own by selecting a backup provider "just in case." Since the backup must be given *some* business to keep him in the loop, a portion of the sole supplier's business may be given to the newcomer, opening the door to more opportunities. Clearly the customer is entitled to hear about the emergency procedures that will protect his investment, even if the possibility of interrupted service is highly unlikely.

For many Israeli businesses, terrorism is the elephant in the room. Whether or not the topic is brought up by anxious customers/investors, it is on the minds of everyone doing business in the country. Developing a contingency plan—if only to relieve the anxieties of the customer—makes good sense. There could be other considerable benefits: First, through the brainstorming of an emergency plan, new ideas for running aspects of the business may occur and actually become the standard. Second, by sharing your contingency plan with your customer, you are inviting constructive criticism that may contribute greatly to your operations. Third, your plan may force your competitors to counter with their own backup procedures, which is good for the industry and maybe even good for you in the event of an actual shortage. And, finally, a contingency plan will, some sleepless night, relieve *your* anxieties as well.

THE COMPETITIVE ADVANTAGE OF BEING "DRIVEN"

When Eyal Kaplan stated that every Israeli businessperson of his acquaintance felt driven to show the investors who turned their backs on Israel that they have made a mistake, I couldn't help thinking that such a defiant attitude is a "benefit" of sorts from the terrorist crisis. Would that all managers and workers felt this way! Of course, Israel is a country at war, and it is predictable that there would be a sense of unity and defiance in the workplace, just as there had been in the factories of Russia, England, and America during World War II. But a company does not have to be situated in a war zone to benefit from the passions of its employees. American workers are not, at the time of this writing, living in a country besieged by terrorists, yet periodically *customers* turn their backs on the products and services they strive so hard to provide. Is it out of the question that a company's workforce should feel slightly offended when the customer chooses—all things being equal—the competition's product? Would a dash of defiance be so bad?

Kaplan was suggesting that Israeli businesspeople take rejection *personally,* and that they react by, in effect, proving the customer wrong. Most American CEOs would, no doubt, love to have an organization that responded to defeat similarly. A company with a rank and file spurred to excellence because of wounded pride would be a formidable competitor, indeed. Managers should not shy away from helping to promote a healthy defiance in the workplace, as opposed to a philosophical "win some, lose some" acceptance of fate. For one thing, it is a lot easier on the manager. A workforce that is "driven" needs less supervision, because it tends to be self-monitoring. Managers who can light a fire, not under the butt, but in the belly of their subordinates will have created a team that has something to prove to the world.

Accordingly, managers should not stand by and watch the wind fall out of the corporate sails after a major contract has been lost. It is time, of course, for a pep talk, but not simply to raise flagging spirits; the workers must be reminded that they have been wronged. A customer has looked them over and decided they were not up to the task. That customer must be shown the error of his ways. How do you prove to the customer that he has made a mistake? The lost customer has competitors—sell to them. The lost customer is part of an industrial community made up of companies that talk to each other—establish a reputation of excellence within that community. The lost customer was trying to do what was best for his company—go back to him and let him know you are still a resource. The lost customer will continue to face new and evolving challenges—update him on every advance of your technology. Always be a David in attitude, even though you may be a Goliath in assets.

SIMULATING THE SENSE OF "GROUP"

Business fraternities in Israel do not have to be institutionalized. As Eyal Kaplan made clear, one's circle of friends doesn't change; it just keeps expanding. This became abundantly clear to me as I continued with my interviews in Tel Aviv and Jerusalem. At each new appointment, I made a point of mentioning whom I had previously interviewed. Invariably, the response would be: "Ah, I know him (or her) well; we are old friends." And I couldn't help thinking that this network of friendships, or at the very least, acquaintances, must not only be a great comfort during times of crisis, but must also accelerate the pace of business considerably. One of the most time-consuming formalities in the American business community—the introduction of companies, followed by the qualification process—is unnecessary for the most part in Israel, where a great many businesspeople already know each other and have worked with each other, or know someone who has. Contracts are sometimes dismissed, as two lifelong business friends swap services or goods. The nature of competition is altered; it is not easy to drive a competitor who sat next to you in third grade into the dust. In an economy under terrorist attack, cooperative actions can be agreed upon over a phone between CEOs, without the "assistance" of the HR and legal departments. There is also a poignant side to this efficient network: Just about everyone in Israel knows a victim of terrorism. The commuter killed on the bus by a suicide bomber is not a stranger and not a statistic.

What Eyal says about America—the land of the individual—rings true. It's probably safe to assume that most business professionals in the United States do not, on a regular basis, do business with childhood friends. One could go further and generalize that, statistically, few Americans remain in close contact with their grade-school playmates. And although there are certain benefits to living a professional life well outside the circle of one's early acquaintances—such as the ability to act the executive when there is no one in the company who remembers the time you peed in your pants on the playground—it can be lonely in urban America during a crisis. Speaking from personal experience, I can remember driving through the streets of Los Angeles amid the riots following the Rodney King verdict and envying the solidarity of the Korean business owners, whose extended families protected their stores from looters when there were no police to be seen on the streets. The average Los Angeles business professional looked a lonely figure, indeed, behind the wheel of a locked car, as he apprehensively made his way, inch by inch, out of the city via jammed freeways.

The Israeli sense of fraternity can be simulated to some degree. Professional associations, such as Rotary or Kiwanis clubs, chambers of commerce, and hundreds of industry-specific groups, can make the shyest among us feel as if we belong to a community that offers friendly advice, moral support, referrals, and even direct business opportunities. In times of economic trouble, or worse, the friendships forged in such organizations can buoy the spirit and rally the common cause. Should terror visit the United States again, business relationships will mean more than the occasional golfing foursome. One's group can become a survival mechanism.

CHAPTER ONE

Checklist for Managing a Business Under Fire

- ❑ Plan for flexibility.
- ❑ Search for opportunity in a crisis.
- ❑ Remember the importance of word-of-mouth advertising.
- ❑ Redefine your market.
- ❑ Take your business case to the owners/investors.
- ❑ Share your contingency plan with your customers/investors.
- ❑ Remember the competitive advantage of being "driven."
- ❑ Simulate the sense of "group."

CHAPTER TWO

Meeting the Threat

■ ■ ■

"I learned how inefficient we were before this crisis. When business returns, we'll make a fortune here. We'll never go back to the old ways. The intifada has been a school for us."

—*RAPHY WEINER, GENERAL MANAGER, DANIEL HOTEL*

THE RESPONSE OF THE ISRAELI BUSINESS COMMUNITY TO THE terrorist crisis was not uniform, for a number of reasons. Primarily, no one thought the intifada would last longer than previous terror campaigns, which typically wound down within two or three months. Second, terror affects various industries differently. While the tourist industry was immediately and gravely threatened, high-tech companies, which already have issues unrelated to terror, were confronted with problems with a longer fuse—the eventual loss of customer or investor confidence, for example. Even within a given industry, companies took different measures to deal with the economic depression, although all were variations on the theme of survival. Some hotel owners, for example, implemented radical changes to their organizational flowcharts and service offerings; others refused to change. Both schools of thought were able to claim success because "success" was being defined as "survival, and a bit more."

As we drove to one interview, Yoram worked his cell phone (ubiquitous in Israel) to reschedule or confirm the next appointment. Some of the conversations were in English, and I could hear him argue, cajole, and in some cases shame a CEO into granting an interview. Not everyone wanted to discuss such a sensitive topic with an American writer—one from Los Angeles, yet—with no pro-Israeli bona fides, who was not even Jewish. Yoram tried to invoke the authority of the Ministry of Industry and Trade, winking at me as he assumed gravitas. Nonetheless, there were executives who would not talk to any writer who was an unknown entity. This, I realized, was the other side of Israeli fraternal solidarity: the insular, self-protective side. Given the treatment Israel is often given by the press, I couldn't blame them a bit.

Fortunately, Janos Damon, director of the Israeli Hotel Managers Association, was to come to the rescue. I had contacted him through an e-mail, then met him on one of his trips to Los Angeles. He immediately contacted his associates in Tel Aviv and Jerusalem and vouched for me and the project.

Thanks to the advocacy of the ministry, Yoram's extraordinary familiarity with virtually every business leader in the nation, and a good word from Janos, I was able to meet with just about anybody I wanted. This chapter includes my interviews with, among others, the CEO of Israel's largest hotel chain, the CFO of the largest metropolitan bus company in the country, and the founder and president of one of the nation's most successful high-tech companies.

Interview with Ami Hirschstein, CEO, Dan Hotels Corporation

"Whoever bases his decisions on the future will not come to the future."

Now that we were off the freeway and in the city of Tel Aviv, our driver Kobi was somewhat restricted in the speeds he could attain—if not by inclination, then at the very least by stoplights, traffic, and the buildings that loomed in his path. Sudden bursts of speed, necessary to the daring maneuvers that were the spice of Kobi's life, were followed by much braking and impatient finger drumming on the steering wheel. As we made our sporadic progress through the streets of Tel Aviv on a beautiful winter day, I was struck by the apparent normalcy of city life. The coffee shops were crowded; the buses were packed with commuters. The scene did not appear all that different from the streets of Los Angeles. Even the sense of awareness evident on the faces we passed did not strike me as unusual; people are aware in L.A. as well, albeit for different reasons.

Ami Hirschstein, CEO of Dan Hotels, is a distinguished executive who moves with the economical grace one sometimes sees in the elderly. His office, atop one of the exclusive Dan Hotels in Tel Aviv, is perched over the Mediterranean Sea. Shafts of sunlight streamed through the lighthouse windows, illuminating his white hair and white shirt, so that he looked like an apparition behind his desk. With the proprietary air of a man accustomed to a million-dollar view of the sea, he rose and shut the curtains. No longer an apparition, he seemed every bit the CEO, in command of the biggest hotel chain in Israel. He has been in business since the birth of his nation. He has seen the economy take many a dive, through the War of Independence, the Yom Kippur War, the Six Day War, the Lebanese War, the Gulf War, and the Iraqi War, to name a few. But this most recent intifada (there have been two previous) is, because of its duration, the worst he has experienced.

Hirschstein: When the intifada began, I had a feeling it would be long term—not three or four years, that surprised me—but I thought it would last six or eight months. And eight months was "long term" in light of our previous experiences. I was very worried, because eight months of 30 percent occupancy would mean bankruptcy.

I thought it was important to define the situation. We held an association meeting of hotel owners; everybody wanted to talk about the effect of terror on the tourist cancellation rate. But to me, the cancellation rate wasn't the whole story. I've lived through lots of wars here, and people don't necessarily cancel; they just don't come—they're no-shows. What counted was the occupancy rate.

So we all made predictions. I predicted the occupancy rate would drop from 85 percent to 30 percent. This was very early in the crisis, remember, and some owners laughed. As it turned out, it dropped even lower.

Q: Were the actions you took, then, different from those of your associates, the other hotel managers?

Hirschstein: Very much so. Because many didn't think the terror would be sustained.

Q: What did you do?

Hirschstein: Here's what we had: thirteen hotels, 3,200 rooms, 3,500 employees. We fired a thousand employees, immediately. After two months, I checked income against expenses and saw that we had to reduce the layers of management. The assistant managers were let go. It was very difficult to do this, because these were the managers of the future. Then the existing managerial staffs were cut in half, and we reduced the head office by 35 percent.

For operational and morale purposes, it was important to reduce numbers at each level—not to send only the Indians home, but also the chiefs. Each chief costs as much as twenty Indians. Some departments we closed completely; some we merged with others. Managerial salaries, including mine, were cut 30 percent. The employees worked in proportion to the occupancy. If we were half full, they took home half of their salary.

We did this immediately, in October 2000, while the rest of the hotels didn't react until March the following year. It's not enough to know what to do; one has to act. The other managers thought this might be a temporary situation and thought it unwise to send even part of the professional core home, because this was the foundation for the future of our industry. I told them, "Whoever bases his decisions on the future will not come to the future." That was my slogan for the company.

Yes, I know it sounds harsh. But that was the way it was. We were in the greatest crisis of our industry. Immediately after the intifada, occupancy dropped from 85 percent to 50 percent. Then, one week after the bombing at the Dolphinarium [see the interview with David Cohen and Zeev Keren in Chapter 4], occupancy dropped from 50 percent to 25 percent. Then it dropped even lower: We had hotels with 300 rooms with maybe 30 or 40 rooms occupied.

My main concern is the cash flow. There was a lot of investment before the intifada because projections for the incoming tourist flow were very optimistic. Most of the hotel chains here owed maybe a hundred million dollars to the bank. Nobody could pay back the principal, but we had to at least pay the interest.

Q: How did you motivate the employees and managers who remained? Weren't they afraid they would be fired next?

Hirschstein: Let me answer that backwards, because only smiling, motivated employees will provide the best service. So how was our service? With reduced salaries and reduced staff, and with all the uncertainty of the times, our guest-satisfaction rate has not dropped.

My definition of service is: "to meet the expectations of the guest." And those expectations are different in various hotels. You can't compare the service of a luxury hotel to the service of an inn, or the service of a resort hotel to a city hotel. What I wanted to do was give the guests a little bit above their expectations—not a lot, because that would mean bankruptcy, but a little. And I wanted it to come as a surprise.

I'll give you an example. An American executive arrived here one morning. Because of jet lag, she went straight to bed. About two o'clock in the morning, our operator at the front desk saw that she had begun making phone calls. Of course, everything is closed in a hotel at two in the morning. The operator called room service and sent up a pot of coffee and some cake. The waiter knocked very quietly on her door; when she opened it, she was given this tray of coffee and cake. She wrote me a letter afterwards saying that she had stayed at hotels all over the world, but she had never been given such thoughtful service. For thirty cents, she'll remember us forever.

Now, I'm getting to your question: What about the employees? I wanted them to be aware enough, like that front-desk operator, to give our guests a little bit more; so we had to give *them* a little more as well, and that, too, had to come as a surprise. For example, we'll give our housekeeping staff a little party or a trip to the country, or even a little scholarship for the children of exceptional employees. We authorized every manager to give $60 bonuses to no more than ten employees a month. It wasn't much, but you'd be surprised to see how it makes their day.

Another way to motivate my employees is to involve them so that they feel as if we are all—executives, managers, housekeepers, and cooks—in the same boat. We hold monthly meetings to explain to the employees what is happening and exactly what they can expect and what they cannot expect. Accordingly, nobody had false expectations.

The meetings were two-way. We invited criticism. At first, people were afraid to talk, but when they saw there would be no repercussions, they participated. One housekeeper, who took care of the eighteenth floor, told us that several times a day she had to ride the elevator down to the basement to get a drink of water. The time it took for her to ride down and back up again, several times a day, was ridiculous. All we had to do was put a water cooler on every floor, but we never knew that until she told us.

We all had the feeling we were in this crisis together, and everyone contributed with ideas to save money and keep the service up. And there is always this to remember: We took care of our people before the intifada. When the intifada happened, our people paid us back.

Q: I spoke with Ari Marom earlier, who told me the Ministry of Tourism changed its marketing tactics after the terror began. Did you do likewise?

Hirschstein: We realized no one was going to come from abroad during this period of violence, which has lasted now nearly four years. So we spent the money on the local market. The local market was not ours; it belonged to our competitors. We had to penetrate that market while cutting our expenses. But the marketing is not all local. We contacted the decision makers in the Jewish associations, in the United States, and in the evangelical movement in the Bible Belt.

Q: How do you square not basing decisions on the future with the importance of being prepared for "the day after," when the tourists return?

Hirschstein: There is no "day after." I don't believe that something will happen that will suddenly put us where we were. But there will be a point of change, where the down arrow finally stops its downward path and turns in the other direction—*this* is the time to start advertising and reaching out for the tourist markets, and this is the time to start slowly preparing yourself for the return.

I think we are at this point now. There may not be peace, but I'll settle for nonwar. True peace may be generations from now, made by people who have forgotten our differences.

Q: You've been in this business forever, but I'm sure you're always learning. What have you learned during these last three years?

Hirschstein: That you can do the unbelievable. No one ever thought you could run a hotel with 25 percent to 30 percent occupancy. If you asked a CEO in an American chain if it was possible, he would think you're crazy. But we are doing it.

■ ■ ■

THE IMPORTANCE OF DEFINING THE PROBLEM

Ami's point about the importance of defining the situation, as fundamental as it may sound, cannot be taken for granted. There are managers, even in Israel, I discovered, who do not put "terrorism" up on the board along with all of the other obstacles a business plan is designed to overcome. Some managers I interviewed gave me the impression that, because it has gone on for so long, terrorism has become, in their minds, like the weather, not subject to personal control. It is also a difficult topic to introduce without fear of being associated with negativity. No one wants to stand before a board of directors or an audience of investors and give the impression that one's business is under siege. The prospect of long-term harassment by murderous fanatics is not something one wants to bring up before people who are only concerned with the return on their investment dollar. Even on a personal level, it is difficult to acknowledge the hatred of others. Who among us would just as well *not* think about an implacable animosity out there, directed at us simply because of who we are?

Another variation on the understandable temptation to deny the problem is to mentally place the threat somewhere other than in your neighborhood. A number of managers joked with me about the extreme wishful thinking of some Israeli friends of theirs. To make themselves feel safer, they will, for example, acknowledge the terrorist problem—but in Jerusalem, not really so much in Tel Aviv. Or in downtown Tel Aviv, but not really so much in the suburbs. Or, yes, in the suburbs to the west, but not really so much in the east, ad infinitum.

Ami Hirschstein's insistence on immediately defining the problem makes perfect business sense. The issue of terrorism is a business challenge, and challenges are generally reduced to less intimidating proportions during brainstorming sessions. If the projected strategies of a competitor, for example, are put up on the board, why not the projected actions of a terrorist group? Both require contingency plans. The terrorist is, after all, one's competitor from hell, who is out to destroy one's capacity to operate a bus company or a hotel, restaurant, airline, or tourist agency. And there are actions the business community can take against the competitor from hell, which we will examine in Chapter 5. Terrorists, for example, can be effectively sued; their goals can be thwarted through strategic business investment in cooperative enterprises across the borders; and their victory can be denied by every business success. The precursor to finding the solutions, however, is to define the nature of the problem. Ami Hirschstein faced the gravity of the situation months before his contemporaries and therefore gained a "head start" on the path to redesigning the Israeli hotel to operate efficiently with drastically reduced occupancies.

FOCUSING ON TODAY

"Whoever bases his decisions on the future will not come to the future." Could there be a more disconcerting company motto? Can you imagine a commercial for General Electric or Intel beginning with

a corporate policy statement that says, in effect, "We live day by day"? Certainly, a CEO who stood before the board of directors announcing a doctrine of extreme short-term focus would not inspire the confidence of stockholders, who are accustomed to the presentations of "visionary" corporate leaders—unless, that is, all concerned were in a fight for their very lives. There can be no more fitting testimonial to the seriousness of the emergency in the Israeli business community than when the CEO of thirteen of Israel's most prominent hotels tears down the pie charts on the wall pertaining to long-term projected returns on the invested dollar and reveals his strategy for surviving *one more day.*

It was during this interview when I realized, with another pang of fear, that this crisis was happening to what could be any American company. Aside from a few irrelevant exceptions—such as the preponderance of instant, not brewed, coffee, and the fact that everyone writes backwards, from right to left—Israeli companies are virtually indistinguishable in form and function from their American counterparts. Here I was, in the penthouse executive office, atop a beautiful hotel. Everything was so familiar, so substantial, so "American"—everything except the mind-set of the determined man in front of me. I have interviewed business leaders before who have "turned the company around," to the delight of the shareholders. But, as great as their achievements had been, the miracles had been performed in a peacetime economy; the poorly performing companies in question were anomalies, surrounded by prosperous companies. The man I now interviewed had been in a protracted four-year battle; the entire economy in which he struggled had been the focus of repeated attacks on civilians. The terrorist crisis had narrowed the corporate "vision" of this prominent CEO, and of all of his contemporaries, to day-by-day survival. If it could happen in Israel—a mirror of Western business mores, practices, and values—it could happen in any country, including my own.

Much can be learned from an accomplished business leader who finds his back against the wall. The problem, I realized, was in the transmission of the message. It's one thing to read, for example, about a mountaineering technique for crossing a bottomless crevasse and quite another to actually feel the cold wind as one tries not only to cross, but not to fall. Interviewing Ami Hirschstein, I was feeling that cold wind. Here was a highly esteemed CEO, who should have been in his golden years, forced by circumstances into a survival mode. He might as well have been wearing camouflage paint and fatigues. I would have thought, with fifty years of management experience under his belt, he would have been spared this indignity. It was like seeing one's father forced to physically defend himself. But Ami Hirschstein was not handicapped by age; I had the feeling that this crisis had summoned up all the traits that had served him well as a young manager who had taken the Israeli business community by storm. There was absolutely no hint of give in the elderly man sitting across from me. In fact, his long experience in business, and in life, seemed to petrify the resolve never to surrender to the violence and hype of the times. Again, the terrorists had underestimated their adversary.

Suddenly Ami's intonation—"Whoever bases his decisions on the future will not come to the future"—made chilling sense. In a way, it was the advice of an older man who had learned how to live out his days by living in, and enjoying, the present. It was also strategic advice for any business caught in a war against domestic terror. If a general were to base his battle strategy on a grand continental plan, rather than on the imminent threats arrayed before him, the battle could well be lost. The "future" is assured only by successive victories *now*. Despite his protestations to the contrary, Ami was a visionary CEO, indeed.

▪ ▪ ▪

Interview with Opher Linchevski, CFO, Egged Bus Company

"We have been attacked hundreds of times. . . .
We are targeted because we are the biggest."

No Israeli business is associated with the present-day terrorist crisis more than Egged Bus Company. News media images of smoldering, distorted bus frames, in the aftermath of a suicide bombing, have come to symbolize the war being waged against Israeli civilians. The world outside the country may not know that the images are almost exclusively of Egged buses; the terrorists have singled out the largest of the metropolitan bus companies and have spared, for the most part, its competitors. The bombings mostly take place inside the vehicles, but sometimes alongside them (via a suicide car-bombing attack) and sometimes in the crowded bus stop itself. The explosions have been disproportionately powerful to the means of conveyance; one wouldn't think so much power could be packed beneath a person's clothing, but buses have been lifted into the air and body parts have been found a hundred yards in the distance. Hundreds of Israeli citizens have been killed over the past three years, many thousands have been wounded—a large proportion wounded for life. In every case, police, ambulance crews, and passersby rush to aid the injured and the dying. Streets are closed, news crews arrive, and the aftermath of the attack is broadcast around the world. Images of the wounded being carried away, blood streaming from their faces, and of the dead—very often children—lying broken on the pavement, haunt the civilized conscience. Yet the deliberate mass murder continues.

And so does the bus company. Egged runs nearly 4,000 buses a day along 1,300 routes, braking at 20,000 bus stops that are typically 500 meters apart. The company dominates two-thirds of the market. In traffic, Egged buses can be seen everywhere, making the well-meant advice of my wife and friends—"Don't ride the buses"—seem darkly comic. You don't have to literally ride the buses to be in danger; they are alongside you, or in front or in back of your car, or passing by in the opposite direction. Any one of them could be carrying a suicide bomber. The idea that an Israeli citizen, on or off the bus, can protect himself through vigilance is absurd. When stuck in a traffic jam, next to a bus or sandwiched in between two buses, you simply have to play the odds. When dining in a sidewalk café and a packed Egged bus pulls alongside the curb, you continue with dinner. There is no practical alternative to developing a fatalistic attitude, because the danger cannot be escaped.

I was looking forward to this interview because, for the life of me, I could not see how a business such as this could continue to operate, much less make a profit, under such horrific conditions. I was shown into the office of Opher Linchevski, Egged's chief financial officer. In his thirties, he is a very pleasant guy, but uncannily still, in terms of body language. His voice was so quiet I leaned forward straining to hear and felt obliged to call a time-out more than once while I played back the tape recorder for a moment, just to make sure it was picking up his voice.

Q: Of all the companies in Israel, yours has been hit the hardest, and certainly the most frequently. Can you give me an idea of how many times Egged Bus has been attacked in the last four years of the crisis?

Linchevski: We have been attacked hundreds of times.

Q: *Hundreds?*

Linchevski: Yes. In fact, I can give you a list of the attacks, at least for the first year. It's very accurate; we used it in court in our lawsuit against the Palestinian Authority. [See the interview with Ram Caspi in Chapter 5.] We listed, I believe, seventy specific attacks during the first year of the intifada, and the frequency of attacks picked up from there. And, by the way, not one of our smaller competitors was attacked. We are targeted because we are the biggest; we carry slightly over a million passengers each day.

Q: Surely, the volume of passengers has gone down.

Linchevski: Oh, yes, and the effect on the bottom line is dramatic. Our numbers tells us there has been a 10 percent drop in demand, but intuitively, I would say it's more. But let's use the 10 percent figure; that's approximately 200 million shekels [$50 million] a year, while our costs have gone up dramatically. As an example, we hired 500 security guards who go on the buses regularly. That was a major expense.

A bus service is very basic. The percentage of profit in a good year is not very high; it's a few percent. So a 10 percent drop in demand is dramatic. Now, remember, this 10 percent is a baseline. After every bombing, there is *another* deeper drop in passengers. Slowly, demand returns to the minus 10 percent level, which means we are losing 200,000 shekels a year in direct revenue while spending more. All because of the crisis.

Q: Has the security presence reassured the public? And did you announce the implementation of guards with an ad campaign?

Linchevski: Well, we have shown the public we are trying our best to minimize the level of risk. But there is a marketing dilemma; we can't push security too hard. Let's say we run a commercial showing our guards checking the passengers. Okay, people watch the commercial and then confidently board an Egged bus, which is subsequently bombed. You see? There are matters of credibility, and there are legal matters that would arise.

We don't feel comfortable in advertising our security efforts, knowing that there could be an attack tomorrow. What we do is tackle the issue indirectly. We'll show a commercial showing the patriotic side of Egged. We'll show a bus driving through town, and then we'll say something like, "We've provided a service in wartime and peacetime; we were always there."

We will also talk about the reliability of the drivers. And we'll show the difference between Egged and our smaller, nonlicensed competitors. There are thousands of small, nonlicensed buses, vans, and minivans on the road every day, purporting to be a legitimate transportation service. They're not really legal, but there is virtually no enforcement.

We won't say, "Egged is safe," because we don't see an elimination of attacks. Hopefully, what we've done will stop many.

Q: If passengers are afraid to ride, what about the drivers? Are they afraid to drive?

Linchevski: I'm not aware of even one case of a driver quitting Egged due to the situation. How do I account for that? Well, there is 11 percent unemployment, that's part of it. But there are [other] reasons: loyalty, and the refusal to give in.

Some of the buses, which now look like tanks, have to go into dangerous areas. Even these drivers do not resign. Some even volunteer for these routes. We ask, "Who wants to go?" and the hands go up. There is no increase of pay.

Our drivers get therapy sessions, personally and in groups, from clinical psychologists we have hired. [See Chapter 3's interview with Pazit Bernstein.] We also give a lot of training to the drivers so that they can deal with a terrorist attack. This amounts to thousands of hours of both therapy and training. The overall effect is, our drivers feel as if Egged is doing its best to deal with the problem and to take care of its people.

Q: Do managers ever ride along in a bus to show support by, in effect, sharing the risk?

Linchevski: Sure. Some go even further. We have a [board of directors] of eight or nine members; at least two of them that I know of will regularly go out and *drive* a bus a couple of times a week. Some of our managers come to work on the buses, even though they don't have to.

There are other ways to show support, like going to a specific station and talking to the drivers, or going to the hospitals to visit wounded employees, or a lot of other small things.

Q: You mentioned the lawsuit. I'll be interviewing Egged's attorney later in the week, but I've got to ask you: What was it like to look across the room and confront those who defend terrorist actions?

Linchevski: I can admit that on a personal level you almost don't feel it. The guys that I faced were very educated, very gentle. There is a very different feeling in the courtroom [than] from the actual event. The atmosphere in the courtroom is not tense. Secondly, the testimony, in English, must be translated and it lowers the level of tension. You talk in the corridors with these people and you come to the conclusion it might be possible to have peace. You feel as if you are dealing with people you can talk to.

Q: That's good to hear. Does your sense of eventual peace influence your business plan for the company?

Linchevski: We [prepare] our projections both optimistically, based on peace, and pessimistically, based on the ongoing intifada. But, I will answer your question more directly. In 2004, I am projecting zero growth.

Q: Well, that must be a pretty grim meeting with the board?

Linchevski: Well, we are very realistic here in Israel. But, look, it's not all bad. Our business plan is sound, even though I'm projecting zero growth for the year. I'll give you an example.

In the last year and a half, we have started issuing bonds; we've opened the doors to the money markets and Israeli pension and trust funds. To do so, you have to get a rating from the rating companies. The rating is based very significantly on your strategic plan. People want to know they are dealing with a management team that knows where it is going. After all, these bonds have a term of ten to fifteen years. We've received quite a nice rating, AA minus, which is very good for a business like ours; it's one of the highest ratings in Israel.

If a big pension fund, for example, gave us a 50 million shekel loan based on a fifteen-year bond, they agree that Egged will be around for many years. And the interest rate they give us is based on an AA minus, which is not a high-risk premium.

So, we have a long-term strategic plan that has found favor with investors. Then, we cut it into yearly budgets, to factor in the current situation. So the funds that I will have to implement our plan will be less than in good times.

Q: You took over as CFO in the middle of the crisis. Did you have any reservations about going to work, in a very high profile position, for the company in Israel most targeted by the terrorists?

Linchevski: This is a great challenge, but I wanted to come aboard. First of all, it's one of the largest companies in Israel. And it's a private company with funds to do some exciting things. I like to think of myself less as a CFO and more of a business developer. Here, I can think in those terms. This is a time of tremendous opportunity.

We've incorporated a new daughter company, a trucking company, as well as a taxi company, [and we are] entering as partners in the Jerusalem LRT [light rail transit] project. We are also involved in developing a subway system for Tel Aviv. So we've entered the rail business and the small vehicle business. We may have done these things sometime in the future anyway, but it was important for us to do them now, during this recession. The intifada gave us the push.

■ ■ ■

LETTING SECURITY SPEAK FOR ITSELF

This was the second time I had encountered a company that invested heavily in security procedures, but declined to highlight the issue in its marketing campaigns. El Al Israel Airlines—famous for its in-flight air marshal presence, thorough baggage searches, and rumored antimissile defenses—highlights only customer service in its ads. And now the CFO of Egged Bus, having invested in a security force that not only rides the bus, but also drives in advance of the bus, questioning suspicious passengers waiting at the scheduled stops, was not comfortable advertising the fact. Both companies would have found customers eager to hear the message. It's not as if the Israeli public would have been shocked by a company raising the subject of customer security. They would have been delighted. So, why wouldn't El Al and Egged emphasize the precautions they had taken on the behalf of the customer? Not only would the customer be reassured; the terrorist might well go elsewhere.

Amos Shapira of El Al made the point that security will one day become less of an issue. Opher Linchevski did not want to give his customers unrealistic expectations, because it could cost the company credibility and have possible legal implications. Another reason not to spend a lot of marketing dollars on the issue of customer protection might be that security speaks for itself—if the customer can see evidence of the systems in place.

Customer security has always been a touchy subject with American businesses, which are reluctant even to raise the issue for fear of causing anxiety. Security has traditionally been a covert undertaking. Hidden cameras relay images to hidden guards sequestered in command centers far from the public eye. Security officers are often broad-shouldered types, stuffed into blue blazers so they might appear more like customers. Should there be an incident, such as a shoplifter caught in the act, every effort is made to escort the culprit away as quietly as possible so that the surrounding customers remain blissfully unaware. Even Hollywood movie versions of crime on the street always show the detective hero in a three-piece suit, melding into crowds, being as inconspicuous as possible. Uniformed "Sergeant O'Malley" characters are only called in after the fact, to protect the crime scene. Only after the 9/11 attacks has the American public seen police forces on the street, armed with automatic rifles, protecting the cities during especially high terror alert levels. And, generally speaking, the public has been gratified.

Customer security for pre-9/11 America had been heavily influenced by the Las Vegas or the Disneyland models, in which a vigilant, behind-the-scenes, private security force protected an oblivious public. After 9/11, security has come out of the closet. Should there be more terror in America, it won't be long before our companies will reassure customers "the Israeli way." There is no attempt to conceal primary security procedures in the Israeli business community. Guards are everywhere, for all to see. It is common knowledge that diners in Tel Aviv or Jerusalem will choose the restaurant with the guard at the front over one without. Security is ostentatious, for the very good reason that a traumatized public craves to see it. And when obvious security procedures are established, the word gets around. How else has El Al, which does not even indirectly refer to its customer safety programs in its advertising, become synonymous with security? Every passenger can attest to the extraordinary baggage search procedures, which are performed for all to see. At the El Al terminal in Tel Aviv, I stood for two hours in one of ten lines watching every blessed carry-on bag and suitcase painstakingly examined by the hands of very alert security pros. And, considering the high stakes of air travel in that region of the world, I didn't mind the delay a bit. I could see why commercials vaunting security were unnecessary; all El Al has to do is remind the passenger to be at the terminal *three hours* before the flight. The implications are clear.

SHARING THE RISK

One doesn't normally associate riding a bus to work with acts of courage, but there must be days when the passengers, the driver, the guard, and the Egged managers who ride along have to take a deep breath before boarding the bus. There is no predictable pattern to the terrorist attacks, which is, no doubt, a purposively added element of uncertainly on the part of those behind the terror campaign. Bombings are random and sometimes have occurred two or three times in a single day. Some days, however, are more tense than others. Following a pitched battle in the West Bank, terrorist groups publicly vow revenge; the threats are broadcast in Israel, so the community knows all too well the form "revenge" will assume. Israeli passengers, waiting at the bus stop or riding in the vehicle, are alert for suspicious behavior. Many feel an obligation to unbutton their coats so that all can see there is not an explosives-laden belt underneath. Egged bus drivers, some of whom are armed on particularly dangerous routes, have been known to push an entering passenger back out into the street if something strikes them as odd.

How many of us think of a bus or subway commute to and from the office as an opportunity to relax, read the paper, or take a little nap before the workday officially begins? Now imagine the strain of constant vigilance on the Israeli commuter. I asked myself, if I were an Egged manager, would I ride the bus to the office if I did not have to? The "10 percent" of riders Opher referred to have found other ways to get to work—car or van pooling with associates, or group taxi rides. Would I have found an alternative as well?

World War II bombing crews were often surprised by an unannounced visit from a general, in his flight suit, ready to accompany them on a perilous mission. Even battle-hardened veterans attested to a soaring of morale, and perhaps a sense of invulnerability, when the senior officer voluntarily threw his lot in with the success or failure of the mission. Equally gratifying was the "hands-off management" demeanor of the general. Even though he might have had much more combat experience, he did not offer advice unless it was sought; the pilot remained in command. Perhaps the metaphor is a bit of a stretch, but I can easily imagine how much an Egged bus driver might appreciate the company of a manager along a route that had been bombed the previous day. Even more inspiring would be the sight of a passing Egged bus, *driven* by a member of the board of directors. Egged, incidentally, is an employee-owned cooperative, so it is not unusual that a member of the board is perfectly familiar with the mysteries of driving a bus through Israeli traffic.

It is particularly important during a crisis that executives and managers, who form and enforce company policy, have a clear idea of the challenges faced by employees and customers alike. If Egged managers were to avoid taking a bus, their view of the business environment would be based on the field reports of others, intrinsically biased by personality. The manager would have no basis to evaluate an employee's request or suggestion, and no firsthand knowledge of the customer's frustrations or wishes. Ironically, it is probably much more likely for a manager to lose contact with both the employee and the customer during a time of crisis. You might think that a national emergency in itself would be sufficient cause for a heightened awareness throughout the company, but that is not a given. *Egged's customers are being murdered.* Could a manager be blamed for coveting the sanctuary of the office, or for thinking of his responsibility to family before his responsibility to his organization? Wouldn't a "ride along" under current circumstances be above and beyond the call of duty?

Egged passengers, drivers, guards, and managers have no practical alternative. The passengers must get to work; the drivers and guards must make a living; the managers must see for themselves the business environment in which the company operates. I would bet all reassure themselves with the odds: Thousands of buses are on the streets daily, and "only" a couple hundred attacks have occurred over the last four years. Certainly, a vigilant frame of mind can also help reduce the chances of being a victim. And bus-riding Israelis indulge in occasional fatalistic humor. But there is no doubt that all concerned experience the risk, together, on a daily basis. Managers who wish to help guide Egged Bus through this unprecedented ordeal cannot afford to lose touch with those they have the honor to serve.

■ ■ ■

The Bombing at Mike's Place: Interview with Head Chef Nick

"There was a boom and a flash,
and I was suddenly lying on the ground."

We stopped for lunch at Mike's Place, a very well-known bar/restaurant on the boardwalk in Tel Aviv. It had been bombed within the year. Yoram told me it was one of the busiest nightspots in Tel Aviv. Mike's Place also happened to be in the shadow of the American embassy, which was no doubt taken into consideration by the suicide bomber. Right before the entrance stood a makeshift memorial to those who had been killed. Three photographs, probably supplied by friends of the victims, had been pasted to black poster board. One was of a musician, perhaps in his forties, in a kind of reverie with his guitar while playing in front of an attentive audience of young people. Another was of a young man smiling for what appeared to be a spur-of-the-moment snapshot; he couldn't have been over twenty-five. The third photo was of a young woman, her face slightly averted, as if she were speaking to someone off camera; her hair, moving with the turn of her head, covered some of her profile. Below the simple memorial stood a vase of flowers; below that sparrows hopped about the sidewalk. Inside, Mike's Place had a cozy and intimate setting. We stepped into massive wooden booths that offered a degree of privacy. In a separate area, the bar was a long sweep of mahogany, bottles glittering beneath the mirror. As we ordered lunch, Yoram introduced me and asked if we could have a few words with someone who had been there at the time of the bombing.

A young man soon walked out of a back area the swinging doors revealed as the kitchen. He approached our table and introduced himself in a British accent as Nick, the head chef. He was that species of chef that manages somehow to remain as thin as a rail. He gave the impression of having an abundance of nervous energy. I could easily picture him multitasking in the busy kitchen, directing the assistant cooks and keeping tabs of every burner, acting as a kind of culinary air traffic controller. With lunch hour being a hectic time of the workday for a chef, I kept the interview short.

Nick: Seven months ago, a little after midnight, I had finished my shift. The bar was packed, inside and outside. It was one of the busiest nights we've had for a long time. It's normally pretty busy, anyway. This is the friendliest bar I've ever seen. All kinds of people come here—diplomats, hippies, business execs, tradesmen—and complete strangers strike up conversations.

But this was a Tuesday night, when we have our jam sessions. A lot of musicians come here on Tuesdays—nobody famous, just very talented local guys—and a lot of people come to hear them.

I went outside to get my bike, was saying good-bye to someone. There was a boom and a flash, and I was suddenly lying on the ground.

There were two bombers, but only one's bombs actually exploded. Three killed—two musicians and one of our waitresses, who was a sweet kid, twenty-seven years old. Thirty were injured.

Q: Did the bombers just walk in and mingle?

Nick: Our doorman thought the lead bomber looked pretty suspicious. He started questioning him and then pushed him back. The other one got in and blew himself up.

Q: Did you see the bomber?

Nick: Afterwards, yes. Part of him was hanging from the roof.

Q: Was there chaos in the bar?

Nick: Well, we're right next to the American embassy, so within a minute or two there were security and medical people here. Then lots of help arrived.

Within a week, we were open. We had a big ceremony; thousands came. There was a very moving tribute, speeches, tears.

Q: Did the customers return?

Nick: Oh, yes, we're packed every night. I read in the paper a thousand restaurants, cafés, bars have gone bankrupt. But we're as busy as ever.

Q: Have you ever had second thoughts about living in Israel?

Nick: This will sound funny, after what I've just told you, but I feel safer in this country than I ever did in England. In London, there's violent crime every day. Here, it's almost unheard of. I could spend the night on that bench outside and be perfectly safe. In fact [grinning], some of my friends have done just that.

■ ■ ■

MEMORIALIZING THE VICTIMS

We thanked Nick for his time and left Mike's Place, pausing once again at the memorial. Now that I knew more about the story and more about the special ambience of Mike's Place, the tribute to the victims seemed doubly touching. I was ashamed when the practical, analytic side of my brain asked, "Is this memorial a smart move, for a business catering to a clientele in search of entertainment and relaxation?"

There are perfectly understandable reasons why a business would not want to memorialize a violent event, even though the victims had been loyal customers and friends. Certainly, a memorial to those murdered in the establishment would not be a marketing department's first choice of customer inducements. Most restaurateurs would not want to draw the attention of incoming guests to the fact that they are entering a recent crime scene. It's one thing for a proprietor to boast that "Billy the Kid was shot here" 150 years ago, but it's quite another to remind customers that the restaurant they are about to enter has been a recent target in an ongoing war. I don't know how many McDonald's or Taco Bells would be allowed, even if the local manager were so inclined, to memorialize an event that, from a marketing standpoint, should be forgotten. A much more likely recommendation to the owner of the stricken establishment would be to lay the regrettable incident to rest.

The issue of customer comfort aside, employees, too, have to be considered. There is something to be said for the "out-of-sight, out-of-mind" approach. Employees must, after all, smile throughout the business day. Without a constant reminder, the incident could be effectively repressed in a matter of weeks. Moreover, if there's employee turnover, why turn away prospective replacements or bias their on-the-job attitude with a memorial to those whose only fault was being in the wrong place at the wrong time—when *your* place was the wrong place? Although a lovely sentiment, a monument to murdered customers is likely to discourage at least some prospective customers and employees.

This was not the only such memorial I would see in Israel. Café Solel in Jerusalem engraved on its outside wall the names of the eleven who had been murdered while eating their breakfasts. The Dolphinarium, now an abandoned disco, has a memorial to the twenty-one teenagers murdered there. Sidewalk and street memorials at the site of bus bombings could have, I supposed, raised the eyebrows of city fathers who are trying to attract foreign tourists, not frighten them off with visual reminders that they are vacationing in a war zone. But business owners and council members alike continue to pay tribute to the victims of terror.

Sentiments aside, there *is* a business case for memorializing murdered customers. Most importantly, such displays establish one's business as part of the moral struggle against terrorism. What would the community and the existing customer base think of a proprietor who did *not* erect a memorial to the friends and fellow citizens who had been murdered under his roof? Local patronage, I would imagine, would decline, if not cease. A standing public tribute to the dead also says a lot about the owner's attitude to his living customers, who are obviously not just numbers to be rung up on the cash register. Anyone who cares this much about his former customers must offer thoughtful and personalized service. A monument might also, ironically, relieve the tensions of prospective customers. If an establishment has already been bombed, another attack is statistically unlikely (you would have to live in a society under attack to appreciate this reaction). And a memorial performs a public service, reminding passersby, customers, and employees of the establishment to remain vigilant. Years from now, when there is peace, these memorials will say much about the Israeli business community and how it took part in a resistance movement of sorts, alongside its customers, against organized terror.

In many societies, impromptu memorials of flowers and candles are often set up at the site of a fatal car accident. Those driving by cannot help but notice the sentimental gesture. In a city of millions, it may be unlikely that passersby personally knew the victims, but the sight of funeral wreaths laid upon the busy sidewalk in broad daylight is affecting. All are reminded of the hazards of speed and heavy metal, and of one's mortality. At the very least, people make a mental note to be more careful on that particular turn or intersection.

In Israel, such memorials are tragically common—the difference being, of course, that the public's attention is not being drawn to the site of an unfortunate accident but to the crime scene of a deliberate act of multiple murders. Witnessing one such memorial in a lifetime would be shockingly unforgettable, but Israeli citizens have seen dozens over the years. In these cases, it is not a matter of reminding yourself to be more careful in traffic. The horror of these memorials is that the victims were already vigilant at the time of their deaths. Terrorists managed to penetrate the defenses of an aware society, place themselves among its citizens, and—in the instant of their momentary gasp of recognition—kill themselves and anyone near.

How do people cope with the implications of such monstrous crimes? The perpetrator is dead (along with the innocent), so justice in the strictly immediate sense has already been done. Yet hundreds of Israelis—family members, friends, and coworkers—are psychologically wounded after each attack, or they are literally maimed, blinded, or otherwise damaged and traumatized for the remainder of their lives on earth. Across the security barriers, in neighborhoods not far from home, thousands celebrate the event in the street; candy is strewn to the throngs like jewels. Others publicly volunteer to follow the lead of the martyr. Cash payments to the families of the murderers, in sums that amount to a personal fortune in that part of the world, are made by far-off supporters of terrorism.

Israeli employees arrive to work just like anyone else similarly affected by memorials in the street. Many emotions are carried into the workplace—rage, desire for vengeance, depression, hopelessness—all counterproductive, from a managerial point of view. But, of course, the managers themselves feel no different. Not only must they control their own emotions, they must do what they can to help their associates. A manager in Israel must at times be a family counselor, a lay rabbi, a civil defense adviser, perhaps even a babysitter; but managers must also direct and inspire their personnel toward their workplace goals. And the surest way to do so is to remind every employee that the terrorists would like nothing better than to be the cause of an economic collapse.

■ ■ ■

Interview with Youval Rasin, Vice President, BioGuard

"Every customer we have has expressed concern about terror."

These last four years of the crisis have been very hard on Israeli start-up companies because they are unusually dependent on the support of foreign investors, who have been frightened away by the repetitive media images of an economy under assault. These fledgling companies are generally in the high-tech industries. Very often, they are formed by former military buddies who leave their active military obligation with the some of the best technical training in the world. The Israeli soldier is often characterized in newspaper cartoons with a battlefield laptop in hand. Perhaps no other military has so synthesized brain and brawn—the disproportionate investment in brain making the brawn less likely to be put to use.

BioGuard is located in an industrial sector outside Tel Aviv. Youval Rasin, a young vice president, led me into the conference room. I had a glimpse of several offices and saw entrances to a production area in the rear. The place gave the impression of activity and potential. The offices felt crowded, as if the company were already in need of a bigger building. It was the kind of facility a CEO might point to years later with nostalgia, as the site of a burgeoning operation. The interview had been set up on the fly, Bio-Guard having been recommended to me the day before.

Q: Thanks for meeting me on such short notice. Can you tell me a little about your company?

Rasin: We specialize in relating identification documents, like a passport, to the person, using biometrics. Our core business involves antihijacking systems. For example, if someone other than the owner takes over a car, the system can recognize that there has been a change of drivers. It then asks the new driver to identify himself or herself. If they are not in our database, the system actually takes over the car, remotely, and slowly and safely reduces the speed to a standstill.

Q: That might keep my wife from driving my pride and joy. Coming out of the intifada, what have been the biggest challenges for your business?

Rasin: It's very difficult to invite customers and investors to visit the company. They believe what they see on the news, and those reports have been consistently bad for years now. So we don't try to persuade them to come.

And we now have questions from our customers abroad that we never used to hear. They want to know what we will do if there is a bombing. Can we still deliver? Will we keep an inventory? And so on. People are not eager to deal with a company in what they perceive to be an unsafe environment.

Q: How do you calm their fears?

Rasin: Well, we have to show them that this is life here, and that we are able to cope with it. Any instability they see on the news does not threaten, for example, the nature of things. This is not some third-world country where instability can lead to a change of government through revolution or coup.

Every customer we have has expressed concern about terror. I have a speech handy, to put their minds at rest. Yes, a speech. If I wing it, I might forget a key point or two.

Some customers of ours—the ones who have managed to come here—have said they were surprised by the number of soldiers with guns on the street.

Q: After a terrorist attack, do you call your customers, to do a little PR?

Rasin: Not really. We are so accustomed to the terror, we don't think about it much. It happens, and we continue to work. It's not big news.

Q: But it could be big news to your customers. Your customer in Europe might think, "Hey, that bombing was in Tel Aviv. BioGuard is in Tel Aviv. Maybe I should think about a backup plan if BioGuard's operations are affected by terror." So that customer chooses another supplier, just in case. He has to give that supplier *some* business to keep him in the loop, so he takes away 10 percent of his orders to you and gives them to his backup supplier.

Rasin: [Laughing] Okay, I'll call next time. It's probably a good idea.

Q: Have you lost personnel? I don't mean as victims of terror, but good employees who have left the country because of the crisis?

Rasin: Yes, we had a Canadian R&D manager who left the country; his wife was worried sick. She was in Canada, watching the news. This is typical. We can't compete against the news media.

Q: That must be doubly frustrating—to lose a good manager and to have nervous investors—and there's not a lot you can do to counter the media reports.

Rasin: But we learn from the way the news media behaves here. I'll give you an example. We are working on a project in the Ivory Coast. It's been four years and already we've been through two revolutions and two presidents. When other companies left, we stayed. We made the right inquiries; we didn't rely on the news media. We assumed their reports would be much like ours. The truth of an incident is always much smaller than the broadcast and usually limited to a small area in a country. So we stayed through the revolutions. We could hear the shooting in the streets, but we stayed.

Q: Have any of your employees been in a terrorist attack?

Rasin: No, but the country is small. We all know someone who has been affected by terror. I don't believe there is a single person in Israel who has not lost somebody—after twenty years of on-and-off war.

Q: What did you do in the military?

Rasin: I was a captain in the paratroopers and saw combat in Lebanon.

Q: Do you think universal military experience has a positive influence on Israeli businesses?

Rasin: Yes, but it's a two-edged sword. It's very difficult to operate a company when your key people have to go for thirty days' active duty every single year. We plan for it, but it's still a challenge. You can't go out and hire someone for just a month, so we all fill in for each other.

Q: I would think that, for certain products, the Israeli experience with terrorism would be an absolute credential.

Rasin: For security products, definitely. And global acts of terror definitely increase the demand for our product.

■ ■ ■

USING THE EXPERIENCE WITH TERROR TO EVALUATE OPPORTUNITIES

Although no one would wish for it, personal experience with terrorism can be a definite asset when evaluating risk in a foreign country. I thought Youval's Ivory Coast anecdote both amusing and informative. The Israelis, having lived with terrorism in their own country, were not impressed by the news reports of widespread chaos in the African country, nor even by the sound of gunfire in the near distance. Any other businessperson, myself included, would be stuffing clothes into the suitcase. The Israeli contingent virtually yawned through a national crisis in a foreign land while their American and European counterparts fled for their lives. Youval's obvious contempt for the news media as a source of reliable information is clearly based on his experience with the media in Israel. "The truth of an incident is always much smaller than the broadcast." That's the conclusion of someone who has seen for himself the disparity between how the media portrays life in Israel and how life in Israel actually is. Youval simply divided the media's dire predictions by half. Even the sound of gunfire is not necessarily troubling to the Israeli entrepreneur; it has been heard before.

Youval and his associates were able to see the "emergency" in the Ivory Coast for what it was: a semiviolent changing of the guard. The new government immediately assured the foreign businesses, which it coveted as much as the previous rulers, that all was well. The BioGuard team was uniquely qualified to evaluate the situation. They knew from firsthand experience in Israel that there have been no interruptions in production, no failures to deliver, no breeches of contract, and no loss of return on the investor's dollar. Rightfully assuming the situation in the Ivory Coast was being similarly hyped by the breathless reporters, they made their own inquiries and came to their own conclusion. If only more foreign investors applied the same logic to the situation in Israel!

COPING WITH THE NEARNESS OF DANGER

Before an interview with the general manager of Mt. Zion Hotel in Jerusalem, Yoram took me to a viewpoint alongside the road in an outskirt-city named Gilo. "Come, I want to show you something." We stepped out of the car and walked to the edge of the cliff, overlooking a village not more than a few hundreds yards away. A wide swath of dirt and concrete rubble lay between the boundary where we stood and the village.

"That is Beit Jala in front, and Bethlehem to your left. They used to shoot at us from there and lob mortars."

"Really?" I asked, stepping back a pace and looking out of the corner of my eye for the nearest shelter. The distance between Gilo and Beit Jala seemed scarcely farther than a Tiger Woods drive off an elevated tee. I listened to Yoram's matter-of-fact voice recount conditions under which I could not imagine myself or my family living—bullets smashing through living rooms or through the windshields of occupied cars. I recalled news footage of angry throngs in the streets and asked Yoram if those streets had ever been filled with demonstrators. After a moment's reflection, as if he were remembering a particular celebratory scene in the aftermath of a "successful" suicide bombing, he answered, "Oh, yes." The voices, I thought to myself, would be close enough to hear. How could anyone live—or work, or play, or draw a single breath without anxiety—with danger so near? And yet the residents of Gilo, driving and walking by, seemed on solid ground, and no more on guard than the average New Yorker in Central Park (perhaps less so). Once again, I felt in my bones the curious paradox of Israel. In a land under the sharp eyes of opportunistic terrorists, I felt completely safe.

It is no doubt difficult for most Americans, living in what amounts to a nation-continent—its sense of space further expanded by great oceans—to appreciate just how close danger lies to most Israelis. Since its inception, Israel has been surrounded by hostility. Its people must live, and conduct business, in claustrophobic proximity to vocal enemies. Many Israelis go to sleep conscious of a restless threat that's scant city blocks away—reminiscent of early European settlers in Africa, listening to the sound of drums in the night. In some neighborhoods, one's imagination has to be kept in check because TV images of angry crowds surging through streets that lead to one's home do not make for peaceful dreams. Homemade and surplus missiles are frequently fired from the borders into the nation of Israel. Without guidance systems, they rarely do damage, but how many Americans could adjust to random missile attacks, effective or not? The suicide bombers plaguing the Israeli economy do not parachute in from distant military bases; they only have to walk a few hundred yards. Demonstrations in the West Bank, replete with gunfire and threatening chants, can be heard by nearby Israelis on their way to work.

▪ ▪ ▪

Interview with Rachel Goldberg, General Manager, Mt. Zion Hotel

"The biggest disaster is for the hotel owners. They saw their investment going down the drain, and that created a sense of panic."

The Mt. Zion Hotel had the same dusty, blocky, "Jerusalem stone" exterior as most of the buildings in the city, old and new. It is an architectural tribute to the biblical past, enforced by the city fathers. Inside, the lobby was cool, quiet, and opulent. The polished tile floor seemed almost a shallow pool with its sheen of dark color. The wide-angle view of the ancient city was spectacular; human history was on display, just as the geological past is on display from the vantage point of the Grand Canyon. Stone walls, built by successive generations, showed different lines of strata, indicative of the materials available at the time. Many houses below, Yoram explained, were built upon existing houses. An archaeologist could theoretically dig down, through the living room floor of a modern home, to the foundations of a Roman wall. Taking it all in—the panoramic view and the exquisite interior of the lobby—I felt great sympathy for the owners of the hotel. With all of this beauty around it, the front desk was idle, the lobby empty except for Yoram and myself. It seemed such a criminal waste of luxury and history. By any rational standard, the place should have been packed with excited tourists. Soon a young lady appeared and showed us into Rachel Goldberg's office. The woman behind a busy desk, with a pencil in her hair, rose to greet us. She struck me immediately as intelligent, overworked, demanding, and fair—the kind of general manager for whom someone would go the extra mile.

Goldberg: We've had bad times before, like all hotels, but things always improved within a year. This time it's different. How bad has it been? In the third month of the crisis, we went from 80 percent to 20 percent occupancy. Now, after three and a half years, we've edged back to 30 percent. All of the hotels here in Jerusalem are at 30 percent. To show you how bad it is, the Hyatt chain has pulled out. The minister of tourism was assassinated by terrorists at the Hyatt. And, generally speaking, they've been hit harder than some other hotels because their location is farther from the center of the city.

The ripple effect is enormous, because Jerusalem is especially dependent on tourism. For every hotel employee, it is estimated there are five other workers in the community dependent on the tourist trade. When we fired 3,000 out of 6,000 hotel employees in this city, the effect was out of all proportion to the actual number let go. Souvenir stores, restaurants, laundries, print shops—all suffered.

But the biggest disaster is for the hotel owners. They saw their investment going down the drain, and that created a sense of panic, which they succeeded in passing on to their managers, who had to decide how much of it they [would] pass on down the line.

I've heard hotel managers joke about how safe it is, today, in Jerusalem. After all, a bomber wants to kill people; but, look, there's nobody here, the lobbies are empty.

Q: Does Jerusalem have a reputation for being more dangerous than other parts of Israel?

Goldberg: Sure, because so many attacks have occurred here. Not only were the tourists afraid to come to Jerusalem, out-of-town Israelis were afraid. The fear was out of all proportion to the reality. If we needed, say, a refrigeration technician from Tel Aviv, he would express fear of coming to Jerusalem. That's because he watches the news.

A friend of mine, a psychiatrist, tells me that people need a place they can perceive as being more dangerous than where they are. Jerusalem became that place. We heard people from the territories tell us they were afraid to come to Jerusalem. Our reaction was: "What? We're afraid to travel *where you live.*"

And, of course, this crisis affects more than Jerusalem. Many, many people are afraid to come to Israel. That's why there are commercials for the hotels in Eilat [at the southern tip of Israel] that do not even mention Israel, as if Eilat were a little paradise in the Middle East that doesn't belong to a country.

Q: Doesn't an increased security presence calm the guests?

Goldberg: Yes and no. It's like flying. The safer you make flying, the more afraid people are to fly. All these security procedures, while necessary, are fear inspiring. People think subconsciously that if they can just go in and sit down in the plane, it must be safe; but if they must go through seventeen different security checks, it must not be safe.

Q: What were some of the first steps you took to cope with the low occupancy rates?

Goldberg: We had to deal with drastically reduced revenue. So, how do you save? We had to cut and cut. But simply cutting back on expenses can be dangerous. It's very easy to destroy a hotel's reputation and very, very hard to earn it back again. We had to become more efficient without lowering the quality of our service. In order to survive, we had to reengineer, to change our operations and cut costs, *without the guests knowing.*

But then, eventually, you have to look at where there is still money to be made.

Q: And where is that?

Goldberg: Well, we had to decide with whom we are going to compete. Our traditional competition has always been the four-star and four-and-a-half-star hotels here in Jerusalem, although there is no longer the "star" rating. These hotels are larger than ours and can better afford to lower their prices. We knew that we could never win a price war with them, no matter how low we went.

So we decided to compete against the hotels that were previously slightly above us—the five-star deluxe hotels. So we had to invest, to become a deluxe hotel ourself. We upgraded the menu and spent a small fortune renovating the lobby. A number of five-star hotels also engaged in major upgrades during the crisis.

Q: Was that a hard sell to the owners?

Goldberg: We are lucky. Our owners are very smart; they agreed to raise the level of competition. Other hotels, with other owners, had different approaches, mainly to drop room prices dramatically.

Q: Did you change your marketing approach?

Goldberg: We had to evaluate who *is* coming, and we had to husband our resources, which are small, and use them intelligently. We had to define where our business was coming from and where it's worth spending money. Where it isn't worth spending money, you have to put the marketing on hold.

For example, tourists traditionally have come to visit Bethlehem. But today, you never know when it will be safe. Sometimes you don't know until that day. The Catholics have more or less stopped coming; they'll return when Bethlehem is once again open and safe. Germany used to send over 300,000 tourists a year to Israel. And they are no longer coming. The Germans are very sensitive to peace and quiet. But the Evangelical movement from the United States, and even Germany, is coming. So we market to them.

As a nation, however, Israel is terrible at PR. The government has always been slow to recognize the value of tourism, and now that they do understand, they have less money to spend on marketing.

Q: You mentioned your owners are very understanding. But they also look to you to lead the hotel through this crisis. When you stand before them and present a business plan, are they satisfied?

Goldberg: You can't lie to the owners, and the situation is pretty bleak. But sometimes the encouragement goes the other way. I see my owners investing not only in this hotel, but in other properties here in Jerusalem. And I know they're smart. That makes me feel good about the future, too.

So, how do I plan? My way of budgeting is to look at the best case, and the worst case, and to try to plan something in between. Budgeting is based on occupancy, and you don't know what your occupancy is going to be. You have so little control. I was talking to a hotel owner in Belgium who told me he makes a five-year plan, *and it happens.* Here in Jerusalem, during this crisis, you plan and then make decisions afterwards.

Q: Will some of the changes you've made remain in place, even when the crisis has passed?

Goldberg: Long-term slumps create changes that will also be long term, even when things improve. In this particular crisis, we've learned methods we'll never get rid of.

I'm always asking, "What can we do *now* that is good when we're empty, that will also be good when we're full?" So we design a reception area that allows you to deal with the customers, using fewer staff, and we do room service out of the bar, rather than having a room service kitchen. But these changes will mean more efficiency even when occupancy rates return to normal.

Q: Is planning for the "day after" a challenge?

Goldberg: I don't believe there will be a sudden change for the better. Look at world history over the past hundred years. There have been lots of sudden changes; they've all been bad. The good changes are gradual. Why should it be different this time?

I used to think about the day after back in October of 2000, when I thought this crisis was a temporary thing. But it didn't go away. The day after has come already, except that we didn't recognize it. We're now dealing with different clientele—most of us work more with Israelis than we ever did before—and we market differently. Tomorrow is here; it's just a different tomorrow than we thought would come.

RAISING THE LEVEL OF COMPETITION DURING A CRISIS

Rachel's business plan, which called for a significant investment in order to upgrade the hotel at the same time revenues had dropped by 60 percent to 70 percent, must have initially raised some eyebrows in the owner's accounting department. Many other Israeli hotels were not only suspending scheduled renovations, but reducing, not increasing, services. A number of hotel owners, advised by competent financial advisers, were thinking of *closing* for the duration of the crisis. Surely, you could argue, the greatest crisis ever to hit the Israeli economy was not the time to implement a grand strategy of taking on the venerable flagships of the tourist industry, such as the King David Hotel, Inbal Jerusalem, Hotel Jerusalem, and the David Citadel.

But a case can be made for raising one's sights during an economic depression. From a practical standpoint, this is precisely the time to upgrade one's image. The renovations for Mt. Zion Hotel, for example, were doubtless less expensive than they would have been in a dynamic economy. The cost of renovations can also be very negotiable during an economic crisis, because many local contractors are hurting for more business and banks are competing for customer share in a shrinking market. The tourists who *do* come to Israel do so with their eyes wide open; most would understandably associate deluxe accommodations with increased security. The proposal to substantially upgrade would appeal to visionary investors, who eschew the siege mentality and, having decided to enter the higher realm of competition, would want to keep pace with the deluxe hotels that were also upgrading. And finally, the decision to increase one's stature is an excellent forward strategy; when the crisis passes, one won't be in a position of having to regain former glory. The Mt. Zion, for example, will be well ahead of the game as a firmly established five-star hotel while the balance of its competitors, having lost loyal customers through reductions of services, will be starting from scratch to rebuild clientele.

■ ■ ■

Interview with Danny Halpern, Financial Consultant

"It's hard to do things by the book when it comes to terror. Terror is still a new phenomenon, and the book has yet to be written."

Before my interview with Danny Halpern, I did an Internet search by typing in his name. The results were quite impressive. His name appeared on executive committees, government advisory groups, as an author, and in media interviews. Danny is a former economic adviser who has spent much time in Washington, D.C. Yoram and I had a chance meeting with him at Café Moment (which had been bombed a year before). After he had set up the interview, Yoram was very pleased. "It's not easy to sit down with Danny Halpern," he told me. "You are lucky." A few days later, Danny sat and swiveled in a chair across from me. Energetic and incisive, he also gave me the impression of being simultaneously shrewd and thoughtful—a combination of intellectual talent I do not often see.

Q: As a consultant, you must work with many investors. What is their perspective on the crisis in Israel?

Halpern: It could not have happened at a worse time. It would have been tough without it, after the high-tech collapse. Then comes the intifada. The partners, investors, and customers from abroad used to visit Israel frequently. Once the news images of bombed buses hit the television screens, they stopped coming.

I was in Eilat recently to meet with an international company that agreed to come, but only in Eilat. Do you know Eilat? It's on our southern tip. There are many beautiful hotels there. Many of them, when they advertise, don't even mention Israel. They have created an impression Eilat is a fabulous kingdom, a Shangri-la in the desert. That is how they defuse the terror issue. I am sure there are tourists in Eilat who do not know they are in Israel. Anyway, these customers asked to be secluded within the hotel. Their plane was on the tarmac the whole time, ready to fly. Ah, you laugh, but this was a great improvement, because for two years they had refused to come at all.

Q: If they're afraid to come personally, aren't they also fearful of putting their money here?

Halpern: The onus is on the Israeli businessman to prove to his customers that, should there be a crisis, he can still deliver. We had to prove this, incidentally, during the first Gulf War. So we have to show our customers that software and even production tools have been transferred to the States, or some other safe place, as a backup.

Every Israeli businessman has to be ready to answer questions from investors about how he has prepared for interruptions to his production schedule. The question, "What happens if?" becomes much more serious today. Investors ask more questions about vulnerability now. When you go to the bank, they ask, "What happens if?" Therefore, the margins that the bank will look for will be wider than the safety margins, because the weight of the unexpected is growing; it's looming bigger.

So, the reliance on local investment versus outside investment has grown in the last few years. A lot of companies prefer to go public in Israel than in the United States, because the Israeli investors are not asking the what-if question to the same degree as an investor in Europe or in the U.S.

Q: These investors expect a dog-and-pony show, however, and a sound business plan. How hard is that, today?

Halpern: A business plan today with numbers that might have appeared in 2000, our best year ever, would raise a red flag with any investor. They would think you're trying to hoodwink them.

We have to be very conservative with our projections, and the investors have to learn to live with them. If these projections do not encourage investment, such is the price we pay. But at least we're dealing with the truth.

When it comes to planning long term, Americans are the champions. But Israelis are much better than Americans at improvising. When terror strikes, you have to improvise. When you live with terror, you have to change course fairly often. But I don't want to give you the impression that this talent for improvisation is reactive; it can also be aggressive. When you are better at dealing with the unexpected, you're better at making the most out of an unexpected opportunity.

Q: Isn't there a drawback to improvisation? I mean, "going by the book" can save a company a lot of mistakes.

Halpern: I agree, but it's hard to do things by the book when it comes to terror. Terror is still a new phenomenon, and the book has yet to be written. A friend of mine works for McDonald's. She is amazed by how thick their manual is. But I doubt if there is a chapter on how to deal with a suicide bombing. If someone pukes on the floor, there is an action plan.

Q: You've spent a lot of time in the States. What are some of the differences between Israelis and Americans?

Halpern: I think Americans are much more risk averse. More Americans canceled trips to New York immediately after 9/11 than did Israelis. I remember when I lived in Washington, D.C. I was driving to the embassy and I almost had an accident. You know why? Because I heard on the radio that the principal of a high school in Oregon canceled a field trip to Washington, D.C. because of the *Achille Lauro* incident. Can you believe it?

The average American plans his summer vacation a year ahead. If something happens in Israel, he cancels and changes his plans. Then, if things quiet down in Israel, it's too late to come here because his new reservations are now in Hawaii.

If tomorrow by magic the Twin Towers were reopened, how many people would rent office space in it? Here, in Israel, we repopulate the café right after it has been bombed.

Q: I'm not sure if I agree. If you look at the sporting events—for example, the baseball playoffs right after 9/11—the stadiums were filled. Americans didn't change their way of life.

Halpern: Yes, but the remedy to terrorism in the United States will have to be more convincing than it is here. If we have one guard in front of the mall that has been bombed, America will put ten guards before the people are reassured. The security will have to be ostentatious. Here, I believe we invest more in the quality of our security people and less in the mechanics. In America, because of the huge numbers, the investment is in the mechanics—the system—and then they hire minimum-wage security staff. Here it's the opposite.

Q: Isn't that one of the areas where being an Israeli company is a definite credential?

Halpern: Yes, we have companies here developing escape mechanisms for people on the hundredth floor of a high rise. We have somebody developing a helicopter rotor that will allow it to fly very close to the sides of a building. We have people here who will be advising the Olympic Committee in Athens.

Q: Do you do business with companies in the West Bank?

Halpern: I'll tell you a funny story. We were having some work done on our house by a carpenter who lived in the West Bank, a very good carpenter. One day he told me he must take a couple of days off, for a celebration. I asked him, "What kind of celebration?" He told me his son was getting out of an Israeli jail for throwing a Molotov cocktail into a crowded bus some years ago. The next week the carpenter asks me if I would mind his son joining the team, here at the house. It was not an easy question, but we finally said yes. He came and did a good job. Oddly enough, he had learned pretty good Hebrew in the jail.

Sometime later, the son was getting married and my wife and I were invited to the ceremony—in the West Bank, mind you. The carpenter met us at the border and we got into his car, because going in an Israeli car would not be healthy. So, off we go to the wedding. Did my wife and I have fun? Yes, we did.

■ ■ ■

MITIGATING THE WEIGHT OF THE UNEXPECTED

Although one could argue that the nation of Israel is always on a state of high alert, with regard to terrorism, there *are* times of increased tension. Occasionally the Israel Defense Forces (IDF) has targeted very popular, charismatic terrorist "godfathers," whose subsequent deaths have led to widespread, extremely vocal demonstrations and well-publicized promises of unprecedented reprisals. Exactly what form the "revenge" will take is always unknown, but there is little doubt among Israelis that in a short time something very bad will happen inside the country. At such times, the "weight of the unexpected" hangs like a pall over Israel. As much as the business community insists upon keeping its normal routine in spite of the political situation, I would imagine business activities might be subdued during the mounting anticipation of a major terrorist action. Such are the subtleties of a terrorist campaign: Just the threat of an attack can create enough anxiety in the community for business owners, investors, and customers to step back and wait for a better time to act.

The ways in which a proactive Israeli businessperson helps to mitigate the weight of the unexpected might be of service to those of us who must await lesser crises, yet feel equally compelled to take whatever control possible—not of the pending emergency, for that is impossible, but of our customer's perceptions of the emergency. If we can positively affect the way our customer views the unfolding events, the actual "big event" will have lost much of its power to influence the customer's decision. In fact, if we can effectively educate and motivate customers, they will have made their decision without *waiting* for the emergency to materialize, convinced that, whatever happens, there will be no change in their business relationship with us.

It all begins with an appreciation of what the least initiated may be feeling during a period of high tension. An Israeli "veteran" of the terrorist crisis, for example, might be so accustomed to the cycles of violence that he may forget for a moment that others—his customers and/or investors—are scared half to death by repeated news reports of ever-increasing terror alerts, terrorist threats, government precautions, and emergency procedures. The first thing the wise Israeli businessperson does is reach for the phone, make contact with those who are important to his business, and walk them through the probable sequence of events, so that they not only know what to expect, but also realize such things have happened many times before during the history of their business relationship.

Communication is everything! Anyone who has ever flown through severe turbulence on a passenger plane can recall the great relief when the pilot's calm, lazy drawl announces things might get a little "bumpy" for a while and that everyone should fasten their seat belts. On the other hand, if there is silence from the flight deck, we immediately assume the pilot is too busy to talk, because he is desperately fighting for control of the plane. The truth is, of course, that the pilot is yawning through the turbulence in either case, knowing full well the plane can withstand forces ten times as great. But if there is no communication, the imaginations of the passengers run wild.

The best way to mitigate the weight of the unexpected is to render it irrelevant. And once customers are given the proper perspective, it *will* be irrelevant; they will be confident that, whatever may come, there will be no change to the enduring business relationship.

CHAPTER TWO

Checklist for Managing a Business Under Fire

- ❑ Define the problem.
- ❑ Focus on today.
- ❑ Let security speak for itself.
- ❑ Share the risk.
- ❑ Memorialize the victims.
- ❑ Use the experience with terror to help evaluate opportunities.
- ❑ Raise the level of competition during a crisis.
- ❑ Mitigate the weight of the unexpected.

CHAPTER THREE

Managing Through the Crisis

"We understand that we have to excel and be better than in more normal times. We can't allow the red lights to start blinking in the minds of our customers."

—*MOTI BONESS, PRESIDENT, ISRAEL AIRCRAFT INDUSTRIES*

THE TERRORIST CRISIS IN ISRAEL DID NOT COME AS A COMPLETE surprise to the populace, unlike, for example, the attack on the Twin Towers. Israeli citizens have not known a sustained peace since the U.N. created the nation only three generations ago. And it seems as if every parent or grandparent has lived through two or three wars. This recent crisis is different, however, in two respects: 1) the obsessive targeting of Israeli citizens and 2) the duration of the terror campaign. Both distinctions have had a profound effect on the Israeli economy and, certainly, on Israeli society.

At the time of this writing, Israeli citizens have endured four years of repetitive terrorist attacks. If the residents of New Jersey, Israel's equivalent in size, had been subjected to hundreds of mass murders over a similar period of time, imagine the traumatic effects upon the populace, not to mention the economy. The business executives and middle managers and supervisors of New Jersey companies would have unique challenges in leading and inspiring their personnel to the high levels of performance all companies require. The business communities of the surrounding states and the outside world would no doubt sympathize, but they would still have to compete against New Jersey companies. It's not as if a terrorist crisis would afford a business special considerations in the marketplace. New Jersey would have to compete just like any other state, but with the added handicaps of a devastated tourist trade, an across-the-board retreat of venture capital investors, a boycott of New Jersey products in some parts of the world, and soaring security costs at home.

It is one thing to mobilize and meet the threat of an emergency and quite another to continually live with the emergency, year after year. An emergency is, after all, supposed to be a temporary challenge; you don't expect it to become a way of life. Experience tells us the storm should eventually expend itself. When it does not, it is no longer a "storm"; rather, the conditions of life on Earth have drastically changed. This chapter examines some of the long-term effects the terrorist campaign has had upon the Israeli business community, as well as the strategies developed in its defense.

■ ■ ■

Interview with Moti Boness, President, Israel Aircraft Industries

"We weren't going to let the terrorist situation force us into a fortress mentality."

Israel Aircraft Industries is a $2 billion company and one of the largest, if not *the* largest, company in Israel. IAI provides parts and systems to the most prominent aerospace companies in the world. President Moti Boness is sixty, ramrod straight, and very fit. Brightly framed photographs of commercial airliners, jets, and missiles line the walls of his executive office. He graciously put his calls on hold and gave me his undivided attention.

Q: IAI has been around for a long time and has been through wars and recessions before. Has this intifada been a significantly different experience, for the company and for the country?

Boness: The terrorist crisis has not affected IAI in a direct way, because we export 80 percent of our product. In Israel, the tourist industry has been devastated, and there is a lack of foreign investment. But we are more dependent on the world economy than on the Israeli economy. Our people are more concerned about the U.S. economy than their own, because that is where we sell.

In indirect ways, though, we have been affected. We have fewer visitors, which is very unfortunate. The [U.S.] State Department has put out a warning not to travel to Israel. The news reports are grim. Our best marketing tool is for people to come and see what we are doing in the way of innovation; this is something that cannot be taken to a customer; they really have to see it. We can make all kinds of presentations and DVDs about what we are doing, but the only way for customers to really appreciate the exciting things we're doing is to come and see for themselves. Since the crisis, the immediate reaction on the part of our customers has been "Let's meet in New York." And we can't insist on them coming here.

Q: Have any come? And, if so, are they surprised by what they see in Israel?

Boness: Oh, yes, some come. Not many, but some. We had some very important customers come, in their own plane. They were very apprehensive, and going to stay just for the day. Their plane was on the tarmac ready to go. But I could see they were beginning to relax as the day passed. I offered to take them to dinner—not in a corporate dining room, but out into the city, at a nice restaurant. I guess they expected the city to be deserted; they were amazed that the restaurant was crammed with people, talking and animated. After dinner, they decided to stay the night. After lunch the next day, they decided to stay another day.

You know, I get very angry at news reports that suggest that Israel is unsafe. Companies that no longer travel to Israel have in a way given in to terror. I could say the same thing about New York: "Two airplanes crashed into the World Trade Center. It's scary to live here. You better not come." But would that be true?

Q: Do your customers fear that, because of the crisis, IAI might not deliver?

Boness: We are a sole-source provider to some of the biggest aerospace companies in the world. And we have never missed a delivery date. We tell our customers, "We'll inventory more, for your comfort level, but look at our record." Yes, today we have the intifada. But before that we had the war in Lebanon. Before that, we had the Yom Kippur War, and before that, the Six Day War. And still, we never missed a shipment.

But it's all a matter of customer perception. We understand that we have to excel and be better than in more normal times. We can't allow the red lights to start blinking in the minds of our customers. If we are delinquent in a delivery—even if it has nothing at all to do with the terror situation—our customer may associate the two.

I will call our customers once in a while, after an attack, for example, to put their minds at ease. We . . . feel obligated to do it, before they raise a concern. The reverse is also true: After a terrorist attack, I may get phone calls from our customers, who express their sympathy and support. It's very touching.

But, you know, there is a great irony. Just as Israelis get used to the terror attacks, *our customers* become accustomed to the terror attacks and are less concerned than before.

Q: Do you think, in a way, that Israelis have gotten too accustomed to the terror campaign?

Boness: Yes, and it frightens me. Thirty years ago, if there was a bus bombing, the nation would go into mourning. The entire country would be in shock. It would take five or six weeks for the dust to settle and for life to return to normal. Today, it's just another incident; we move on. We have gotten used to it. And I hate to see it. But I suppose the more you continue with your normal life, the more you are winning the battle.

Q: Has IAI been able to continue its normal business life, or have you made changes in response to the terror?

Boness: We have reengineered, but not because of the crisis—in spite of the crisis. In other words, this was something we had planned on doing, and we weren't going to let the terrorist situation force us into a fortress mentality. We knew we had to be a better company to compete on the global market. We could not afford to let terror stop us from being our best. So we instituted the Lean Initiative. It wasn't just about cutting costs; we established a whole new corporate culture.

We established four values and their priority, rather than sticking with the traditional values of profit and loss, cash flow, etc. We defined four values in this order: 1) people, 2) customers, 3) innovation technology, and 4) one company.

This last one is important. We are a very large company, involved in a product line that includes commercial and military aircraft, missiles, launchers, satellites, radar, even boats. So you can imagine our organizational structure reflects this diversity, with many divisions and departments. We found that these departments were competing against each other for resources, capital investment, and R&D.

So we had to get people thinking in terms of one company, not just their own division. Sometimes the optimum is the corporate optimum, rather than the division's. That means that managers may have to sacrifice their own success for the benefit of the whole company.

Q: You have 14,000 employees. Have any of them been victims of terror? And, if so, how does IAI help?

Boness: In Israel, we're all in the same boat. Furthermore, it's a small boat. So, yes, many of us know victims of terror. If they work for IAI, the first thing you do is forget about the company hierarchy; it could just as easily have been you wounded in the restaurant or on the bus. That employee is, then, your brother, your friend. The only difference is, as a manager, I may be able to help more. I can go up line and get permission to use corporate resources to help that person. And, I can tell you, that permission comes like this [snapping his fingers].

Q: What if the victim is another company—one of your competitors? Would the rest of the aerospace competitors circle wagons?

Boness: When there is a crisis, there are no competitors. I think that's true in America, as well. If something happened to Boeing because of a terrorist attack, I'm sure Boeing's competitors would come to their aid. It could just as easily have been one of them.

BECOMING ACCUSTOMED TO TERROR

Behavioral scientists may differ slightly on how much time it takes for a new pattern of behavior—such as dieting or exercising—to become firmly established as habit, but the consensus is that it takes a rather short amount of time. After something like twenty or thirty days, it is no longer a matter of changing behavior—by then you are supposed to become a new and changed person. I wondered, as I heard Moti Boness's concerns about the impact of the intifada on the populace, what effect a *thousand* days of reacting to violence might have upon a person's psyche, and what changes might be wrought.

There is certainly something heroic about a populace becoming accustomed to terror. The Western nations, about to be caught up in World War II, were inspired by beleaguered Londoners, who refused to surrender during the prolonged blitzkrieg carried out by the Luftwaffe. The British displays of courage and good cheer must have been a source of tremendous frustration in the war rooms of the Nazi high command. "When," they must have asked themselves, "will these people capitulate?" One imagines the terrorist groups, waging war against the Israeli civilian populace, being similarly frustrated. When your target group becomes accustomed to the campaign directed against it, the repetitive nature of the attacks is almost self-defeating; they seem only to inure.

On the other hand, becoming accustomed to such a horrendous situation is a profoundly tragic adjustment. Just as it is painful to see a chronically ill loved one eventually come to "accept" her disease as a new reality, it is painful to watch a society adapt to random and repetitive acts of mass murder. And not just Israeli society. The spectators, too, become inured. All who watch the news reports of yet another bus or café bombing must admit to becoming accustomed to such outrages "in that part of the world." To paraphrase Moti Boness, we no longer stare in shock at the images of Israeli dead, strewn about the street in the aftermath of a bus bombing. After years of covering the intifada, even the media has difficulty mustering the sense of urgency once appropriate to these breaking stories.

I must say that I was surprised, during my interviews with Israeli executives, managers, and small business owners, by the lack of anger expressed, and by the philosophical resignation that must have taken its place sometime during this crisis. I've taken into account the fact that people will talk to an interviewer and a stranger in a much different way than they will talk to their friends and neighbors. Nevertheless, it was an impression that did not leave me. And I couldn't help speculating on the managerial challenges "becoming accustomed" to the situation might present. Not that the workforce would be zombie-like; on the contrary, it would be vigilant, able to recognize signs and portents of terror heretofore below the "radar." But certainly, much spontaneity would be gone, the smiles would be fewer, and the outlook for the future would be less than optimistic. If that were the case, it would be very challenging for managers, themselves victims of terror, to instill a long-term vision for the company and for the careers possible within it.

High performance requires high morale. If the conditions outside the workplace do not contribute to the well-being of the employees, then the conditions *within* the workplace must. Your office, factory, or warehouse can be a better place than the environment in which the employee lives; it can be safer, and it can be happier, while retaining its identity as a locus of production. "Work" has traditionally been the antonym for "play," and managers all over the world have considered it their responsibility to crack the whip in order to enforce an ethic on employees who would rather be elsewhere. But, when people arrive on the job already psychologically fatigued, does it make any sense to hammer them with reminders that they are there to produce and perform? When the workplace is better than the outside environment, employees will respond with energetic gratitude. Managers can create these conditions without spending a dime; it's not a matter of amenities, but of solicitous leadership. The manager who expresses care and moral support, and who shows by example what must be done "on the job," will be followed with enthusiasm. And the workplace that celebrates birthdays, promotions, seniority, and sometimes just life in general will attract and retain its employees, especially in times of crisis.

GAINING COOPERATION AMONG COMPETITORS

It is a given in business that market share is gained at the expense of your competitors. But it is also true that most companies are driven as much by their competitors as by the demands of the customer. If the customer desires a product feature that is not offered in the industry, there is less incentive on the part of the vendor to invest in the R&D to fulfill that wish. Should the vendor's competitors be working on providing that feature, you can bet the principal vendor, too, will suddenly try to please the customer. Competition in the marketplace puts the customer, who can choose from any number of alternatives, on a pedestal and the vendor at the customer's feet. Under normal market conditions, the survival of the fittest is determined by the patronage of the customer. If a company "goes under," it is usually because the customer exercised his free choice and chose another. No one mourns the loss of one less vendor, nor should he.

Under abnormal conditions, such as the terrorist-inspired economic crisis in Israel, the loss of a competitor is not a triumph for the surviving companies—not if that competitor is driven out of business as a result of terrorism. There is every incentive for competitors to join in a common cause while under terrorist assault, and to even come to the aid of another, rather than let the terrorists have their way. First and foremost is self-interest. If a competitor is driven under by a common enemy, how does it profit the survivor? If Egged Bus Company were to be ruined—and we should bear in mind its smaller competitors have been generally spared by the terrorists—its closest rival, the Dan Bus Company, would ascend to the dominant position in the marketplace. Would the terrorists, having tasted victory, inexplicably stop their campaign? Or would the new king of the hill, heretofore less frequently targeted, find itself in a worse predicament—saddled with an influx of customers it cannot properly serve *and* under terrorist attack?

As we have seen, Israeli managers know each other personally, band together in associations, communicate during the crisis, and are aware of each other's challenges. It is not unusual for hotel managers, who are in earnest competition, to help each other with needed supplies, bedding, or even temporary staff in the event of a sudden arrival of very welcome guests. Should one of the hotels become a direct target of terror, it is very likely all other hotels would come to its assistance. The owners and managers realize that each successful operation is, in effect, a bulwark in the defense of the economy. Should there be a breech in that defense, all the remaining hotels would become more vulnerable. A hotel "going under" in normal economic times would perish by the rules of the game; when one is driven out of businesses through terror, the rules have been broken and the game itself is threatened. By not coming to the assistance of a competitor damaged by terror, one is implicitly helping the terrorists. And, if by some arbitrary pardon, one hotel were to be unmolested throughout a campaign against the others, it would not inherit the fleeing guests. The tourist industry would collapse just as surely. Like a medieval castle standing tall in the midst of impoverished villages and fallow fields, it could not draw sustenance from its surroundings.

Interview with Mickey Schneider, General Manager, Sheraton Tel Aviv

"We all went to a university, where they teach how to run a hotel or a business. But no one teaches you how to run a hotel during a reign of terror. We're doing things that are not in the books."

The Sheraton Tel Aviv is, like the other luxury hotels I visited in Israel, impeccable. The very opulence of the lobby, overlooking the private beach, gives one a feeling of privileged sanctuary. Mickey Schneider breezed through the lobby, shaking hands with guests, flashing a dazzling smile to the staff, and introduced himself to me as the hotel's general manager. In dress and manner, he was the personification of civilized urbanity. He gave me the impression of a casino owner who would gallantly return some of the losses to a bankrupt player. He raised his hand, and a young woman appeared with a tray of coffee and tea. The glasses were crystal, like the chandelier above her. Everything seemed too beautiful, too sacred in a materialistic sense, to ever be disturbed by human affairs. Yet I knew of two suicide bombings that had occurred virtually next door, at Mike's Place and Café Bialik. It seemed an impossible contradiction.

Q: I appreciate this interview. I'm trying to meet as many people as I can in the tourist industry.

Schneider: [Laughing] What tourist industry?

Q: Is it that bad?

Schneider: I was on a conference call yesterday with other managers in the chain. I heard a manager in Rome who was hysterical because his occupancy fell from 85 percent to 75 percent. And here I am at 26 percent occupancy.

Q: Have you been able to reengineer and soften the impact of that kind of drop in guests?

Schneider: Oh, yes. Our headquarters in Brussels can't believe the numbers we are showing. Once our break-even point was 45 to 50 percent occupancy; now it's 26 percent. So I'm breaking even today. Hey, it's been worse. We had months, during the Gulf War, at 11 percent occupancy.

You know, we all went to a university, where they teach how to run a hotel or a business. But no one teaches you how to run a hotel during a reign of terror. We're doing things that are not in the books. If anybody had said to me four years ago, when we had 450 employees, that this hotel could stay afloat with 150 employees, I would have said they're crazy. Today, we're doing just that, with almost the same level of service. Look at that planter outside. A few years ago, there would have been more flowers, less green. Now, it's more green, less flowers. But they're real flowers. We haven't stooped to plastic flowers yet.

Q: What were some of the first steps you took?

Schneider: First, I had to convince the owners that they will lose less if the hotel remains open. It actually pencils out that way; it's very expensive to close down a hotel and then reopen. But, more than that, this hotel is a flagship. If you close it, it would be a death knell for the industry.

Then we had to let many people go. There was so much letting go that if I had to see a manager for some reason, I would ask my secretary to call him to come up and tell him, on the phone, he's *not* fired.

We have some older maids who cannot work as efficiently as the younger ones. But we keep them because they know the history of this hotel. When this crisis is over and the guests return, we'll need their experience to guide the younger staff.

Every dime must be approved by a manager before it is spent. We go down into such detail today. I've become an expert on toilet paper—fluffy, nonfluffy, with air, without air. For every purchase order approved by one of my managers, I call the vendor and squeeze some more. It works both ways: Vendors can squeeze me, too, by asking for prepayment.

And then we did a lot of merging of departments, reporting to one manager. Now, that may not sound revolutionary to you, but you must remember that hotels are very rigid in their operations. The bigger the chain, the more important that everyone does things the same way, so that a customer walking into a Sheraton in Bangkok or in New York will have the same experience.

Out in the chains, just about every department has a manager and an assistant. Here in Israel, some departments don't even have a manager, much less an assistant. Our managers now handle two or three departments, without assistants. But the guest satisfaction index remains high.

Q: Are most of the hotel managers here Israeli? Or do some come from Europe?

Schneider: What manager from abroad would want to come to an industry where all the hotels are breakeven or below; where there are terror attacks? We had a new GM fly in from France with his wife.

There was a bombing on the day of their arrival. The wife made reservations *that night* to go back to France. He, of course, went with her. We had another European GM in Eilat. He transferred out of the country. And we understand. It's *our* war against terror.

So, yes, I think you have to be an Israeli. You really have to know the people here to work with them, to motivate them. You'll never have happy guests without happy employees. You have to smile these days—even though there is terror and you have a son in the army. The guests must see you smiling. It's not easy.

Our maids are afraid to ride the bus, so they take a taxi to work. They're taking taxis on a reduced salary! Yet we have the highest employee satisfaction rating we've ever had. It sounds odd, but we've never been closer before. We're really a team now, a family, and everybody feels better about working here than they ever did.

Q: Are there things you do differently now to motivate your staff?

Schneider: A few years ago, we never allowed our employees to use cell phones. Now we do; we want them to be able to phone around and make sure their loved ones are okay after news reports of a bombing are broadcast. We let them sit in unoccupied guest rooms to watch the news. We have to, or they'll be worried to death, and our guests will see it.

Q: The guests are watching the same news reports. How do you calm their fears?

Schneider: We have armed guards, in slacks and blazers, here at hotel. Sometimes we check everybody—not because we're really concerned, but to make all the guests feel more secure. Or we'll close an entrance from the beach to the hotel, even though it's safe, and detour the guests through the front lobby, because the inconvenience makes them feel more secure.

And I watch over them. I feel responsible for every guest that sleeps in the hotel. I'm the captain of the ship. We had a group that went down to the beach for an event. I called the police and asked them to come over and help [with the street crossing], and we posted guards on the beach.

But the bombings frighten them, surely. We've had some that were very close, at Mike's Place. Also Café Bialik. That was such a tragedy. The bartender over there used to work here. She was a beautiful girl who was very badly hurt. After fifteen operations, we had a special event to thank the doctors and to thank those who had supported her. Maybe that made our guests nervous, but we did the right thing.

Q: Good Lord. Yes, that was the right thing. Have you changed your marketing outreach, since the crisis?

Schneider: I tell my salespeople to forget the dreams of bringing in huge groups of tourists. I want them to focus on one client. On days when we've had two suicide bombings, I tell my salespeople to stay home or work in the office. This is a business where you have to smile. How do you smile on a day when there are two bombings? Besides, corporate accounts don't want to see you on a day like that. We have a pretty good idea, from one hit to another, what the drop will be.

And, you know, it's not a matter of just getting more guests. For example, the weekends are the busiest time for local Israelis to come to the hotel. But on a given Saturday, we might tell an Israeli group of twenty that the hotel is full, because if there were no more groups than just that one, we would just be trading money. We know that above a certain occupancy, we have to open another outlet, bring in another cashier, another waitress, another maid, another cook for the weekend. So, although we would have more guests, we would have five more employees and end up losing money.

Q: You have to appear before your owner, I'm sure, and show your business plan. How difficult is that when occupancy is so unpredictable?

Schneider: The budget for next year isn't worth the paper it's written on. Tomorrow morning, the budget changes. We work day by day, check our cash balance, and pay what bills we can. And every hotel in Israel "plans" the same way.

But here in Israel we have other planning sessions that may interest you. During the Gulf War, we hotel managers met with the government and made plans for the worst. For example, here we are a five-star deluxe hotel, yet we made plans to become a hospital—no, not a hospital exactly, a recovery area for patients who have been treated at the hospital emergency rooms and now need a place to get better. We even had a plan, should we overflow, to transfer patients to another Sheraton.

Q: If the danger was imminent enough to plan for the possibility of mass casualties, that must have been a sobering meeting.

Schneider: Oh yes, it was very serious indeed. We had a similar plan for the second Iraqi war.

Q: You mentioned that hotel in Rome, where the occupancy "dropped" to 75 percent. Do you ever wish you were managing a hotel in a prosperous country, relatively free from terrorism?

Schneider: I'll tell you the truth. To be an Israeli working in this industry during these times and passing through this period of history is really a privilege. We're the only modern country with so much experience with this kind of thing. We've had periods of two bombings a day. I'm sure there are third-world countries with similar experiences, but we are modern, and the civilized nations can learn from us.

■ ■ ■

RECOGNIZING THE UNINTENDED CONSEQUENCES OF TERROR

Mickey's comment, "We're really a team now, a family," expressed a sentiment I would hear repeatedly during my interviews with Israeli executives and managers. The sense of unity, of family, among employees and their managers is undoubtedly an unintended consequence of the terrorist campaign. Had the economic depression not been terrorist inspired, it is likely that the bonding within Israeli companies may not have been as complete or as necessary. An economic downturn is, in itself, cause for a concomitant sinking of the spirits of anyone whose salary, benefits, or hours are reduced or who faces unemployment. But when the state of the economy has a malicious cause, personified by the suicide bomber, who in turn personifies the death wish of scores of terrorist hate groups, people respond more to the cause than to the effect. While a depression caused by traditional market factors may make an employee think of jumping ship, a terrorist-inspired crisis has quite the opposite effect: The employees band together in self-defense.

You would think any manager might rub hands at the prospect of a workforce so loyal to the company that employee retention is no longer an issue. Yet Mickey seemed very solicitous of the well-being of his staff. A manager who tried to exploit the loyalty of his employees would probably have a difficult time hanging on to them once the crisis passed. It is not inconceivable that one day, in an otherwise healthy economy, a hotel could have financial problems of its own, making it difficult to meet payroll on time; employee loyalty could be critical to its survival. And, in fact, employee fealty is just as meaningful now, during the intifada. There are persuasive forces competing for the talented manager—spouses who want to relocate to a safer environment for the family, or positions abroad in healthy economies that promise more money, better benefits, bigger staffs, and advancement. Israeli companies are limited by circumstances in what they can offer. Salaries are either capped or reduced, the workload has increased, and the advancement process is frozen in very many companies. In the words of Rachel Goldberg who was interviewed in Chapter 2, "We are all working harder for less money."

With all of the challenges attending a business career in Israel, there seems to be no appreciable brain drain on a national level. And I have to believe that the executives and managers I interviewed were very conscious not only of living through a dramatic period of history, but of *making* history as well. The hotel managers in particular are, with all of their problems, excited and justifiably proud of their unprecedented operational efficiencies. There is no question in their minds that the innovations in response to the terrorist crisis will revolutionize the hotel industry, worldwide, whether or not terror is an issue. Israeli hotel managers are "rewriting the book" on how to run a hotel. In five years, managers such as Mickey Schneider will be industry gurus; counterparts in Europe, Asia, and North America will be almost sorry to have missed the challenges they faced.

I could easily imagine Mickey attending one of the general manager meetings of the Sheraton hotel chain, surrounded by GMs who presented the results for the fiscal year at 85 percent occupancy. Clearly, Mickey Schneider, after showing proportionately similar results at *26 percent occupancy,* would be looked upon with awe by his associates and by the ownership of the chain. The implications for the industry are momentous: If an organization can make a profit under market conditions previously thought to spell bankruptcy, imagine the bottom line in a benign economy! Surely, Mickey and his Israeli counterparts would enter these global management meetings with a certain air of confidence, if not swagger, much like warriors fresh from the front lines about to address cadets. Why would any professional who loved his industry be anxious to leave the very crucible of twenty-first century business practices? I had no trouble believing Mickey Schneider's claim that it was a privilege to be an Israeli passing through this period of history.

■ ■ ■

Interview with Jacob Even-Ezra, CEO, Magal Security Systems

"But for us to stop an intruder is not to stop a thief. Our intruders come here to kill us."

On the way to the next interview, we drove by an Arab outdoor market. Yoram glanced at his watch and nodded his head decisively, as if having calculated there was time enough for his American guest to pick up some souvenirs. "Dan, you want to shop?" He asked Kobi to pull over, and the maneuver was completed with his usual heart-stopping panache. The market consisted of row upon row of dark, cozy shops separated by walls of hanging carpets. Inside, handmade artifacts glittered on shelves, hung from the ceiling, or rested on the outstretched palm of each proprietor I passed.

Kobi had assumed the role of my shopping guardian. He

frowned on each piece of old-world craftsmanship I admired and shook his head vigorously at the announced price. If a proprietor were to ask for 100 shekels (about $25), Kobi would be indignant. He would grab my arm and start to pull me away. "Come, Dan, this man is a bandit!" At which point the owner, equally indignant, would pull on my other arm, defending his price. The conversation would escalate into Hebrew. Kobi and the owner would go at each other, nose to nose, each man grabbing and restraining the other. Suddenly an agreement would be reached. Amid smiles and handshakes, the price would be cut in half. The owner would take the money from my palm as if *I* had been the intermediary and Kobi the buyer, and we would part the best of friends. As pleased as I was with the little things I had purchased, Kobi seemed even happier over his negotiating successes.

Magal Security Systems is located in an industrial area outside of Tel Aviv. The company began as a division of Israel Aircraft Industries in 1968, going private in 1984. Specializing in perimeter intrusion-detection systems, Magal has installed over 10,000 kilometers of what can best be described as a burglar alarm for the outdoors—the big outdoors. Its market share, worldwide, is about 40 percent. I met with Jacob Even-Ezra, CEO and chairman of the board. Jacob is in his sixties, small in stature, with a disproportionately deep, rumbling voice. The man sounds like an old lion. After pouring me coffee, he leaned back and boomed, "You are the boss, ask anything you want."

Q: Is being an Israeli company a credential in your line of work?

Even-Ezra: Yes, of course. I like the way you asked that. I've been questioned by reporters who ask me, "Aren't you troubled that you are benefiting from terror?" And I answer, "Why don't you ask the chairman of Teva Pharmaceuticals [a large Israeli company] if he is ashamed of making a living off of sick people?" It's a stupid question. He is making medicine for the sick; and we are producing antiterror.

Q: Outdoor protection is tricky, isn't it? If the systems are too sensitive, they produce false alarms because of leaves in the wind. If they're too conservative, a bad guy might get through.

Even-Ezra: Our systems are very clever, just like we Israelis. We are very clever—not because we were born that way, but because our environment gives us no choice. If we want to exist, we have to be smart. So we develop very effective outdoor security systems. Why wait until the burglar pries open a window and enters your house? Wouldn't it be better to detect him as he enters your yard?

But for us to stop an intruder is not to stop a thief. Our intruders come here to kill us. So these systems are very important. We ask the army's elite troops to try and defeat them. This is how we learn. If they find a way around the system, we go back to the drawing board and correct it.

Q: Usually I ask companies how the terrorist crisis has hurt them. I don't suppose I can ask you that, since terrorism is probably good for business.

Even-Ezra: Ah, but it has hurt in one respect. Our customers would be ashamed to say they're afraid to come to Israel because they're all in the security business. But many customers and investors are staying home.

Also, we used to bring our marketing people from all over the world here to Israel. Now, their families won't let them come. So we hold our meetings in New York.

Q: Do you think the Israeli companies that have been significantly affected by terrorism, such as the hotels, deserve the moral support of the companies that haven't been hurt as bad?

Even-Ezra: Yes, I do, and I wish more felt this way. I ask my people to fly El Al instead of the other airlines. Since the intifada, we have no more company outings abroad. It was a favorite thing for our employees, many of whom had never been outside of Israel. Now we hold our events here in Israel, where the money is needed.

There's another way to help. We also join with other companies and try to help the community after work. When the community starts to look at you as a leader, you start to act like one. Just as when a child looks at you as a father; you start behaving like a father and become more responsible.

Q: Although your bottom line is not negatively affected by terror, what about your employees? Have any of them been in the line of fire?

Even-Ezra: Yes. You see, here everybody knows everybody. If someone is getting married, we all know it. If someone is murdered on a bus, we all know that, too.

We have psychologists working for Magal who will counsel employees that have been affected by terror in some way. If, God forbid, an employee is killed by a terrorist, we close the factory and we all go to the funeral. Other companies do this, too. Now, if it's a car accident or a death by natural causes, we are sorry of course, but we don't close the factory. But if it is a death because of a terrorist, we close up shop and go to the funeral. If someone is wounded, we give free time for employees to visit their friend.

Q: Does management make those visits as well?

Even-Ezra: Management goes to the weddings and the bar mitzvahs—do you think we would not go to the hospital? We do more. We will visit a family's home when someone is wounded or killed.

Q: Are there days, then, after a terrorist attack, when it's a challenge to motivate your people?

Even-Ezra: When there is a terrorist attack, our people feel better here at work, with their friends, than they do at home alone. During the Gulf War, when the schools were closed, our employees brought their children here. We set up a playground, and some of the mothers supervised. Other companies did this, too.

Q: That's a great gesture to the employees.

Even-Ezra: [Laughing] What could I do? It's not as if they *asked*; they just brought their children. So we set aside a play area and brought in snacks. My employees were able to go to work without worrying about their families.

Q: They must have known you wouldn't exactly turn them away.

Even-Ezra: Well, our people are confident we'll take care of them. And we try to show them we will. I'll give you an example. We had an employee who had personal problems, which led to a nervous breakdown. He spent four years in a hospital. The doctors asked us if we would take him back. We took him back. Well, the workforce sees this and they feel that they are working for a company that might find a place for them, too, if, God forbid, they are injured in a terrorist attack.

The employee outings encourage a feeling of family that we like to cultivate. We also pay full salary during a reservist's tour of active duty, although, by law, the reservist is entitled only to a government paycheck for the month, and it isn't much. Other Israeli companies do this, too. Oddly enough, the government doesn't; their employees get only the reduced salary for the month.

Q: What did you do in the military?

Even-Ezra: I was in the underground during the War of Independence. Mortars.

Q: Do you think universal military service helps the business community?

Even-Ezra: Well, the reserve obligation is a burden to every company, because we lose 10 percent of the workforce for the stint of duty. But there is a plus, too. We have many cultures here in Israel. People come here from Russia, Germany, America, and other countries. Someone who has served in the military has been exposed to these different cultures. They train together, fight together, and have fun together. When they come to work for Magal, which also has many cultures, they have already acclimated. They're also mature. We send in children and get back adults.

Q: Are there certain military specialties you look for in a prospective employee?

Even-Ezra: Mainly, I want to know if he served. If he didn't serve in the military that means something is wrong. I won't take the time to investigate; I'll hire somebody else.

Q: Are all of your employees Israelis?

Even-Ezra: Not at all. I was one of the first to build a factory in Erez, on the Gaza border. After the Six Day War, in 1968, Shimon Peres came to me and asked if I would help in a project. He wanted to build three or four industrial zones along the borders of Israel and the Arab states.

A thousand Palestinians worked there; we employed a hundred in our little factory, and we did very well. One of the supervisors, an Egyptian who lived in Gaza, called me the other day. I haven't heard from him in years, since I sold the factory. He said he just wanted to stay in touch. He has a factory of his own now.

We had that factory for over twenty-five years. And we never had a problem—not one. That doesn't mean we weren't nervous at first. The first week the Israelis came on the job with guns. After a week, nobody carried a gun anymore.

We all got to know each other. I went to their weddings; they came to my wedding and my children's. My wife passed away four years ago. Four Palestinians from the old factory came to the funeral—at some risk to themselves, I might add. They had courage to come into Israel at a time when tensions were somewhat high. And they had the courage to face their own people, who might have accused them as collaborators. But they came to the funeral.

■ ■ ■

MAKING THE WORKPLACE A SANCTUARY

Jacob's description of employees bringing their children to the workplace, with the country under attack, is reminiscent of villagers in the Middle Ages seeking shelter within the walls of a castle or cathedral on the eve of an invasion. In both cases, it is doubtful that the lord of the castle or the cathedral bishop *invited* the local inhabitants; it was probably more a matter of not turning them away.

I tried to think of an example of an American company opening its doors to the families of the employees during a community emergency. I'm sure it could happen, but very fortunately, community emergencies, other than weather-related events, are few and far between in the United States. I think it's a safe bet to assume, however, that in the event of a local crisis, the company's directives to its employees would be to remain at home, not "Come to work and bring the kids." It's equally safe to assume most American employees would not feel comfortable bringing their families to the workplace without asking permission beforehand. The more severe the crisis, the more likely American workers would be inclined to stay at home.

I think the question is, "Why didn't Magal's employees stay home during a missile alert?" Surely, a company with a history of offering moral support to its employees would have been sympathetic. After all, the threat was real: Forty missiles found their way to Israel during that conflict. Presumably, the threat during this episode was acute enough for the schools to be closed, so the families of the employees would have either remained at home or gone to community emergency centers. That the families instead accompanied the employees and showed up at the corporate doorstep unannounced says a lot about their expectations of the company. That the company scrambled to create a play area for the children, without undue liability concerns, says a lot about *its* expectations of the "other half" of the workforce. It is clear, for example, that there was a relationship between management of this sizable company and the family members of its employees. How could there not be, when executives and managers attend the weddings and bar mitzvahs of their employees, go on company outings together, visit the sick or injured in hospitals, call on the households of one killed in a terror attack, and close down the entire operation so that all can attend the funeral? Clearly, these people were not strangers. Clearly, the factory was more than a place to work. "When there is a terrorist attack, our people feel better here, with their friends, than they do at home alone."

The role of the company expands during a crisis. American companies in the hurricane belt or tornado alley are prepared to temporarily shelter their employees rather than wish them good luck on the perilous drive home. But when the "storm" is terrorist inspired, the event and the duration cannot be predicted. Since

October 2000, Israeli companies have found themselves in a more responsible position with regard to their employees. Sometimes the workplace might be a literal shelter, but it must now always be a metaphorical sanctuary for its workforce—if, that is, production quotas are to be met. Distracted, anxious employees are not free to perform at their best. Whatever the company can do to relieve the stress of living under terrorist threat—in the way of facilitating communication with employees and their family members, updating the workforce on outside terror alerts and subsequent developments, and allowing employees to watch news bulletins or go online or visit fellow employees in the hospital—will be repaid by a grateful workforce.

Magal, it seems, had little trouble assuming new responsibilities toward its people because of the existing level of interaction between management and employees. Perhaps for other companies the transition has been more difficult. However, if an organization expects its people to produce while preoccupied with concern for the safety and whereabouts of their loved ones during a terrorist alert, it will be disappointed.

ASSUMING A LEADERSHIP ROLE IN THE COMMUNITY

We have just seen how Magal assumed greater responsibilities toward its employees during this crisis, but the expanding role of the company did not stop there. In reaction to the terrorist crisis—a situation that actually affected its particular business positively—Magal took an active role in community affairs. While no doubt commendable, the business case for "after hours" voluntary community involvement is less readily apparent. Magal's products are highly specialized, designed for the protection of oil fields, storage compounds, even national borders. It is unlikely that the goodwill engendered in the local community would result in orders for outdoor detection systems. Magal's customer base is global; the positive press the company may receive locally won't reach the eyes and ears of its far-flung customers. Nor would the company want to highlight its efforts to aid a community stricken by terrorism;

there were, and are, already too many news reports portraying Israel as a country under siege. And, one had to think of Magal's employees, who were already immersed in the terrorist crisis by virtue of living there. If there are after-hours activities to be done, why not spend the hours *escaping* the crisis through corporate-sponsored recreational activities?

But community outreach may make more business sense during a terrorist crisis than in happier times. A company's efforts may be more noticeable to the community when the government is otherwise engaged with security challenges. And they would certainly be more effective, since corporate resources exceed those of the individual. There is no question that in the worst economic times in the history of Israel—worse for some sectors of the economy and some cities than for others—any help would be appreciated, in virtually any form, whether it's computers for classrooms, clothing and food for the victims of terrorism, or companionship for the stricken. Although goodwill in the community would not be the primary goal, even a company such as Magal, with its global customer base, can benefit from the positive press. Employees are drawn from the community; Magal's activities may attract the best the community has to offer. Local investors will be impressed; city administrators will take note and perhaps be in a position to return the favor one day. When a war is being waged on a community, its collective memory is long. Companies that helped during the crisis, and those that did not, will be remembered.

Jacob's child-father metaphor is worth examining further, in business terms. Just as the young parent who is looked upon as a "father" becomes one, a company that accepts a leadership role in the community eventually becomes a leader in its industry. The assumption of communal responsibility has a transforming effect upon an organization; it may very well find itself accepting leadership roles in other areas as well—in professional associations, industry "codes and standards" committees, and government advisory boards. The example will have been set, furthermore, for other companies to follow, to the benefit of the community and, frankly, to the benefit of the companies themselves. There is no better leadership "night school" than volunteerism. Employees often find themselves in more responsible roles outside the company than within it, and the managerial skills developed while coordinating a volunteer effort will serve the organization well. Internal morale is boosted when employees return from a weekend of helping others, feeling rather good about themselves. Not only have they helped the community; they have contributed to the peace process in this sense: Any actions taken to defend the economy help in the war against terror. A very few companies, like Magal, can combat terror indirectly and directly, through community volunteerism and the products they produce.

While I was considering the transforming effect an active role in the community can have upon a company, the image of Ebenezer Scrooge unexpectedly came to mind. Before his fanciful journey into the past, present, and future, Scrooge was portrayed as a successful, if ruthless, businessman. After awakening to the plight of his fellow creatures, he becomes a beloved member of the community. I suddenly realized that Dickens never really addressed how Scrooge's personal transformation might have fostered positive effects on his *business* dealings. Dickens was as antibusiness as any person with a conscience living in preindustrial London. The conclusion of *A Christmas Carol* leaves us with the impression that Scrooge had become a philanthropist in spite of the negative effects such a conversion would have had upon his business. Of course, it may have been beyond the scope of the story to suggest that Scrooge's business, as well as his soul, would have benefited greatly from his newfound interest in the well-being of the surrounding community. The association of personal profit and communal good works may have diminished the message of that great classic, but it doesn't hurt to point it out here, in a humble business book.

The Bombing at Café Bialik: Interview with Merav, Restaurateur

"After the bombing, the customers stopped coming."

We stopped for lunch at the Café Bialik, a small, intimate restaurant that was bombed in the spring of 2002. Yoram explained that Café

Bialik was named after a famous Israeli poet. It had been one of the most popular cafés in Tel Aviv, with standing room only for six years. My eyes involuntarily searched for signs of the attack, which killed one and injured thirty. (The reader may remember that the young woman who had undergone fifteen operations, and who had been given a party by Mickey Schneider, worked at the Café Bialik.) Outside, a husky-looking fellow sat on a stool near the front door. He had searched my briefcase before letting us through. After asking to see the owner, I watched a woman approach us, smoothing her apron. Merav, I would guess, is in her early thirties; she is slender, overworked, and very gracious. During our talk, she would occasionally look through the front window by our table, studying, I noticed, any large vehicle—bus, van, or truck—stopping at the curb.

Merav: I was at home that night, taking care of my baby girl. I was watching the news. That's how I found out. An old beat-up car slowed to a stop right outside, letting off a young man, then speeding off again. He walked into the shop next door, went up to the bartender–a pretty girl who used to work at the Sheraton–and asked for a cup of coffee. Then he blew himself up, killing one and wounding the girl for life. After many operations, she still is not rehabilitated.

Q: The café next door had no security guard?

Merav: This is so ironic. My business partner had been next door just hours before, talking about that very thing. We wanted to share the expense of a guard who could watch over both of our entrances. And that night the bomber came.

Q: How bad was the damage here?

Merav: The whole separating wall was blown out. It took several weeks to repair the damage. Government insurance helped a little, but it was a hard time. My business partner left me–just walked away. After the bombing, the customers stopped coming. Meanwhile my costs went up. The guard outside is paid a thousand dollars a month.

Q: Is this a trendy business, anyway? I mean, don't the hot spots change periodically?

Merav: No, not that trendy. For six years, this place was filled with people. You can ask your friend, here. Everyone came to Café Bialik. Then, after the bombing, no one came for at least six months. It wiped out my savings, and I no longer had a business partner.

Q: I notice there are people here now. What brought them back?

Merav: I did two things. First, I brought in very well-known musical groups to perform. Of course, they were more expensive. Then I hired a very famous and popular television chef—he is the Israeli version of your Emeril Lagasse—to spend two months here and train my kitchen staff. Pretty soon, we started getting rave reviews in *Time Out*, and the people slowly returned.

Q: I noticed heads turning as that young lady to your left walked in.

Merav: Yes, she is a famous Israeli actress.

Q: Things are looking up for you, then?

Merav: Yes, but I'm still nervous. A few months ago, there was a bombing nearby, but the news reported it as *this* place. When I heard the announcement on the radio, I thought I'd die.

■ ■ ■

RECOVERING CUSTOMER SUPPORT DURING A TIME OF CRISIS

There are other examples in this book of the importance of investing during an economic crisis, but perhaps none is as easy to grasp as this story. One has a little difficulty relating to a million-dollar hotel renovation, although there is certainly no less risk associated with major investments. But Merav's example is given to us in much simpler terms: A young business owner who could hardly pay the rent decides, six months after a devastating attack, to risk it all with the implementation of two significant upgrades. The music I never had a chance to hear, but I can happily attest to the gourmet quality of the lunch we had.

I suppose what surprised me a bit was the *need* to invest in this particular case. I would have thought that the local clientele would have returned within weeks of the bombing. After all, Café Bialik had been the "in place" to go for six long years. Merav did not express disappointment, or hurt, at the lack of moral support from her regular customers, and I'll confess I did not have the heart to ask. But the question hung in the air between us: "Why would Israeli customers, accustomed to the reality of terror attacks, not return to their favorite haunt?" There may be a dark message to business owners everywhere in Merav's experience: Your regular clientele cannot be counted on after a terrorist attack. Certainly, customers present at the time of the bombing would have been traumatized and unlikely to return to the scene of so much psychological pain. But even the customers who were not present at the time may have been traumatized. Certainly, some of the Café Bialik regulars must have shuddered at the thought, "What if I had been there, at my usual table, during the bombing?" And if fortune had smiled upon them for being elsewhere, would there not be a commensurate subconscious fear of returning?

Merav had to win her customers back with enticements that were not necessary when Café Bialik had been the most popular spot in Tel Aviv. That she had to do so must have seemed unfair; she could not have smiled at the same customers for six years without thinking of them as friends. But the consequences of a terrorist attack far exceed those of, say, an accidental fire. Café Bialik had become the scene of a crime, one of a growing number of successful restaurants and bars that have been targeted by terrorists precisely because of their success. Patrons during a reign of terror may not be attracted by the usual signs of customer satisfaction. In fact, a crowded restaurant may, ironically, be one to avoid. And certainly a restaurant that has been bombed is at least temporarily shrouded in the palpable gloom following an act of terror. In those circumstances, even well-established businesses may have to begin from square one in terms of renovation *and* marketing.

■ ■ ■

Interview with Pazit Bernstein, Psychologist, Egged Bus Company

"I don't say, 'Don't worry, everything is going to be okay,' because I don't know if it will *be okay. Nobody knows at that point. In fact, it probably won't be okay."*

I returned to Egged a few days after my interview with CFO Opher Linchevski. I wanted to meet with one of the company's lead psychologists, brought aboard in response to the terrorist crisis to deal with traumatized drivers. Pazit Bernstein was something of a surprise. I had expected the serious, penetrating persona of a senior corporate clinical psychologist—someone to whom I would be drawn to suddenly confide, in midinterview, my recurring dreams. Instead, I sat across a perky, energetic redhead in her thirties. We were joined by a fellow who really *did* fit the image of a mental health counselor—quiet, deliberate, and soft-spoken—however, he was an analyst from the finance department, named Rani Ben-David.

Q: I suppose all managers, in every business, have challenges motivating their rank and file. But I can't imagine anybody having a tougher job than you. How do you motivate drivers for the number-one terrorist target in the country?

Bernstein: It is very difficult. Our drivers are shot at, ambushed, bombed. Many are armed to defend the bus. I work with drivers who have been hit, and drivers who are afraid of being hit. And then there are the 500 guards who ride the buses. Many of them need attention as well.

Q: I've seen photos of some of the buses after a bombing. I don't know how much a bus weighs, but they've got to be over 20,000 pounds. Yet the hulks are twisted and bent like pretzels. How is it any drivers survive?

Bernstein: The terrorists usually put themselves in the middle of the bus so that there is less damage in the front and back. That's why drivers can survive blasts that kill a dozen passengers. But they are often terribly injured.

Q: Are you involved immediately?

Bernstein: With the actual driver, no. He may be in intensive care for days before I can see him. But with the passengers, yes, I am involved. And the passengers react differently. A bus attack can trigger all sorts of reactions.

Coming to a hospital after a bombing, and smelling the burned hair, burned flesh, and burned clothing in the emergency room—it is very sad. Sometimes, there are people who weren't hurt physically, but who saw it, and who are very badly shaken or hysterical.

A terror attack brings out anger, grief, fear, hate, outrage. There's no way for me to stop those feelings, and I don't try to. Instead, we talk about how terrible it is, how frightening it is. I talk, I listen, and I accept. I don't say, "Don't worry, everything is going to be okay," because I don't know if it *will* be okay. Nobody knows at that point. In fact, it probably won't be okay.

So, my first job is to talk with the people there, because the driver may not be in a condition to talk. We ask the reporters to leave so that there are no camera close-ups.

Q: You *ask* the reporters to leave?

Bernstein: [Laughing] Okay, we throw them out.

Q: Do the injured passengers sue Egged? I can imagine the trial lawyers lining up at an American emergency room.

Bernstein: No, they understand we are doing our best and that no one can guarantee safety. We, as a company, have accident insurance, and that helps cover their expenses.

Q: When you get to meet with the driver, what is your approach?

Bernstein: Well, each driver reacts differently, so my approach may be different. But I will ask him questions. What did you see? How did it smell? What did it feel like? Do you remember what the terrorist looked like? Did you know the passengers?

I want to know what the background is for their fear. It sounds funny, I know. You would think the bombing itself would be sufficient reason for their anxieties. But sometimes the bombing triggers other issues that have been suppressed over the years. Either way, many have anxiety attacks, nightmares, and stress syndrome. Different people react differently; some may not react until a year later, [while] driving in their own car. Suddenly they'll hear the explosion for the first time.

Q: And these people want to return to being drivers again?

Bernstein: Some do not go back to driving, but many do. It's like their private war with themselves. Some want to go back, but we find other things for them to do because, after all, it's the bus customers we have to think about. We don't want a person driving who is posttraumatic.

We have a driver who lost hearing in one ear and the eyesight of one eye in an attack. He has a couple of years of posttraumatic therapy ahead of him. But he's back at work now, in a clerical position tailor-made for him. The other drivers can see they will not be cashiered out, that Egged will find a place for them in the event of a terrorist attack.

Then we have another driver who has been through *two* bus bombings. True, we've put him on a different route, but he's back driving.

Q: Are you their main contact during the therapy phase, or does Egged management also get involved?

Bernstein: I'll answer by way of example. A few months ago, I heard about a bombing on the breaking news. An explosion north of Tel Aviv, three killed, a number injured. I knew the number would probably go up as the media learned more. I raced to the emergency room. When I arrived, I met other people from Egged already there: a social worker, a couple of managers, a vice president, and family members and personal friends of the driver, who had also raced to the hospital. You see, they know immediately who is driving once the news mentions the route or the bus number. Later, Egged social workers and managers will go to the home of the driver.

Q: As a psychologist, how have the last three years of terrorism affected life in Israel?

Bernstein: Well, you have to remember the intifada came as a surprise to many Israelis. We were all pretty hopeful for a solution; we felt peace was just around the corner. Then the terror began. How has it changed us? I suppose we're less innocent. We're more skeptical about how everything is going to end. Israel is different now.

In the back of our minds is an obsession with the news reports. We want to know what's going on more than ever before. Nobody walks around thinking that by day's end, his life will be shattered. But, by living the experience of the last three years, very many people feel as if they have less control over their lives. Many of us wake up with a sense that the day may not end happily. And, when it does end happily, we go to bed thinking, "This was a good day."

But we all come here to work, and to survive. Living in Israel narrows your perspective to survival. It's also very hard to plan for the future. You focus on the day, and you organize by movement. You become less heroic, less philosophical, and you focus on the present and not on the future. The managers here are very practical. Their job is to run buses, and that's what they think about. They focus on the everyday tasks of running the buses.

Q: What do you mean by "organize by movement"?

Bernstein: Oh . . . to think while you're acting. Like on the battlefield. We solve the problem as we work. There seems to be very little time to plan. So we're thinking, digesting, moving at the same time.

Q: What about the children? Can you protect them from the knowledge that there are people out there who are very dangerous?

Bernstein: Here in Israel we have an adult childhood. Our children grow up knowing that they could be targets of a terrorist attack. No matter how we try to protect them from the reality, kids talk to other kids. They watch the news; they know what's happening. And, besides, we want them to be aware when they are on the street.

Q: Rani, you've been very quiet. What is the biggest change you have seen?

Ben-David: The biggest "change" for me was the day after the Seder bombing. One day I was in my office, in front of my computer; the next day I was in combat in the West Bank. And not just me. The whole finance department was mobilized. The three of us had to report for duty within three *hours* of the bombing. We were out of the office for one month. The entire finance department. One is a parachutist, one is in tanks, and I am infantry. In the last year and a half, I have spent ninety days in the West Bank.

When I was eighteen, it wasn't so bad. Now I have a daughter, and I'm very afraid.

Q: How does a company run without a finance department for a month?

Ben-David: Others fill in. We were okay.

■ ■ ■

SAYING "NO" TO CLASS-ACTION LAWSUITS

Egged has suffered mightily during the four years of the current intifada, but its experience could have been, from a financial aspect, incalculably worse. Class-action lawsuits on the part of the injured and traumatized passengers could have done to the company what the terrorists have not been able to accomplish. There can be little doubt that endless legal action on the behalf of thousands of litigants and their families, for damages expressed in outrageous amounts as part of a settlement strategy, would have driven the company into bankruptcy. It is certainly not beyond imagination that the passengers involved in a bus attack might be solicited into a series of class-action suits, not in the hope of "winning" but of settling, for hundreds of millions of dollars. It is a wonder that Pazit had only to order newspaper reporters out of the emergency room and not trial lawyers.

There is certainly precedent, regrettably in the United States, for mass tort action against entities that were already reeling from the attacks on 9/11. Almost as soon as the smoke had cleared in Manhattan, class-action lawsuits, many in the capable hands of attorneys who had made fortunes from tobacco and asbestos industry litigation, were in progress. United and American airlines, which faced bankruptcy in the immediate aftermath of 9/11 due to the damages and the weeks of drastically reduced air travel that followed, now confront the prospect of perhaps billion-dollar lawsuits and decades of legal defense costs. Boeing was being sued. The four airport terminals the terrorists passed through were being sued. The airport terminal security companies and the building owners and landlords of the World Trade Center were being sued. Editorials even appeared begging the president not to declare war so that the insurance companies might not be relieved of their monumental obligations. Congress, in one of its rare moments of expediency, approved the establishment of a vast reimbursement fund for the victims of 9/11. The families of those who perished in the collapse of the Twin Towers were awarded an average of nearly $1.5 million each. The only catch was that they had to agree not to sue, and to withdraw from suits in progress. Hundreds of families rejected the reimbursement and signed onto class-action suits that continue to this day.

The establishment of a fund in the billions of dollars for the victims of 9/11 was not without controversy. "Why," wondered the surviving family members of those who were lost in the Oklahoma City bombing, "was there no equivalent action taken on our behalf?" The answer may very well be that there were no businesses to protect. The congressional members on both sides of the aisle realized that a bankrupt airline industry could "finish the job" begun by the terrorists, by plunging the national economy into chaos. The families and loved ones of the victims had to be dissuaded from pursuing legal actions that might very well, after years and years of litigation, have proven unsuccessful if juries found the airlines and others innocent of gross negligence. The somewhat controversial victims assistance fund has managed to reduce the number of class-action suits, but the implications of the American eagerness to sue does not bode well for a country under the continued threat of terrorism. One only has to imagine the congestion and paralysis of the entire legal system, and the overall damage to the national economy, should terrorist attacks become as common in the United States as they are in Israel, each followed by the aftershock of class-action suits. It would be damning, indeed, if the terrorists were sophisticated enough to count on the American penchant to sue as part of the ripple effect of their attacks.

The Israeli bus passengers who were injured or traumatized during a bus bombing certainly could have made some kind of case against Egged. They could have argued that because of its experience over the past few years, the bus company should have anticipated this or that attack and should have taken more effective measures to protect its passengers. There might be just enough of an argument to launch a class-action suit, in the hopes that Egged, with its "deep pockets," would eventually settle and pay off the claims against it handsomely. And Egged is only one of hundreds of legal "targets." Restaurant owners could be sued for the bombings in their establishments. The same goes for shopping malls for not stopping an attack, hotels for not sufficiently protecting their banquet halls—nightclubs, open-air markets, universities, landlords, retail store owners, synagogues. That these legal actions are *not* happening speaks well of the common cause—not to mention the common sense—in the Israeli community. Every citizen understands that he is in a war against organized terror groups who target the national economy, and that crippling lawsuits against hapless businesses, on the chance of settlement, would only aid and abet the terrorists. If anybody is going to be sued, it will be the terrorists.

INSTILLING THE BIG PICTURE

Rani's story of the entire finance department being absent for a month after the Seder bombing makes a dramatic case for an ongoing program of multiskilled training within any organization experiencing a terrorist crisis. His almost-offhand comment that "other people filled in" spoke of a confidence in the system that was startling. *How* could other people, who were presumably already sufficiently challenged in their respective departments, suddenly add the duties of the finance department of a billion-dollar company to their daily responsibilities? The ability to do so—with three hours' notice and for the duration of a month—is not a matter of having a few staff members at corporate headquarters who are "good with numbers." Rather, it is the consequence of in-depth training, and of doubtless familiarity with the highly specialized systems within a notoriously complex department.

Later, I wondered, "Suppose that tomorrow Egged's routing department, or the logistics group, is suddenly depleted?" It's not as if a manager can pick up the phone and ask the local employment agency to send over a couple of folks with years of experience in proprietary systems that have evolved and been tweaked over the years within the company. In some areas, there would simply be no time to bring a stranger to the organization up to speed; nor would it be practical to hire true specialists, assuming one could find them, for one month's employment. In an environment where absenteeism is common because of terrorist alerts (the frequent cause of roadblocks and extensive delays) or actual attacks, a company must have "hot backup" within its own walls. Egged accomplishes this by teaching key employees two jobs—the one for which they were hired and another, should those services be required in an emergency. There is simply no other practical choice, unless a manager is fortunate enough to have a pool of part-time specialists from which to draw.

The benefits of such a training program actually exceed the goal of having emergency backup. Employees who are exposed to the responsibilities of another department begin to see *the other* side of the story, so they become more sympathetic to requirements they may have previously discounted. The employee begins to get a sense of the "big picture" of company operations and can better appreciate the ways in which to contribute to the corporation as a whole. Multiskilled training is not just an "operational" experience. Friendships are made, and employees learn "whom to go to" for help in resolving issues that transcend departmental responsibilities. Subcultures and fiefdoms within the organization—the bane of CEOs who try to encourage a sense of One Company—are suddenly "invaded" by members of other departments who are eager to learn the skills that may come in handy during a crisis. Departments tend to become less insular. Efficiency "secrets," once closely held, are shared with others. Employees begin to feel more valuable to the company (and certainly less bored with their own routines). Should a crisis arise, such as the sudden mobilization of Rani and his associates in the finance department, there will be people to fill the breech.

Interview with Ronnie Fortis, General Manager, Hilton Tel Aviv

"During the intifada, the pressure to change was very strong. We decided not to change."

Ronnie Fortis was a change in demeanor, and in managerial philosophy, from the urbane luxury hotel general managers like Chen Michaeli and Mickey Schneider. He reminded me, in looks and carriage, of a dean of an English preparatory college—the kind of patriarchal figure the unruly boys might simultaneously fear and respect. In his sixties, he struck me as physically and psychologically unbending. He gave a curt nod to Yoram, whom I thought shook hands with him the way one of the unruly boys, now grown up, might have done. Yoram turned to me and grinned. "Ronnie was once my antiaircraft battery instructor."

Q: Yoram tells me you took over as general manager here at the beginning of the intifada. Did you have enough experience in this particular hotel to react quickly?

Fortis: I'm not sure what you mean by "react." When the crisis came, we lost clients like everybody else. However, the ones who did come were loyal customers. They would either come here, or they wouldn't come to Israel at all. They would not go to other hotels.

I know there were great changes here in this industry. Many hotels cut their prices. Customers could now go to the same room for half price. The pressure to change was very strong. We decided not to change. We didn't lower our rates. We didn't adapt by altering our product.

Q: I'm sure it's not as if the managers who did lower their prices were suddenly at full occupancy. Every hotel, I gather, was pretty desperate for guests. But you felt no inclination to compete?

Fortis: We had just spent $60 million on renovations when the intifada struck. So we had to recoup some of that investment. But we did not enter the bidding war for guests. Many hotels dropped their rates but did not make more money. Worse, the quality of their product went down. When that happens, you lose your loyal customers.

Our average rate did not drop a penny. To make 30 percent on $200 is much better than making 50 percent on $100. I would rather argue with a client about price because I can defend our price with service. I never want to argue about services we no longer offer, because it's a lost battle. Once you cut services, you can't just snap your fingers and bring them back.

Our competitors were able to make a little money by cutting costs and lowering their rates. We were able to make a little money by keeping our rates and service the same, and cutting other costs. In the long run, we keep our reputation for service. Reputation is very easy to lose and very hard to regain. [Shrugging] We have a different philosophy.

Q: What about marketing? Did you change your focus?

Fortis: The only reason a corporate account is coming is because he has a good reason to come. I don't have to persuade him it's safe to be here. The pure tourists were not coming.

Q: What about the guests who were already here—were there times you had to reassure them about their safety?

Fortis: There's nothing you can do about a terrorist attack. It happens, and you continue about your business.

Q: But don't your guests look to you, as captain of the ship, for reassurance after a nearby attack?

Fortis: If they do, they see me going about my business, unalarmed.

Q: Ronnie, I feel like a newspaperman looking for a headline quote and not getting it. You must have made *some* major changes in response to the crisis.

Fortis: [Laughing] Okay. Here's your story. The other hotels were lowering salaries, and the unions, appreciating the depth of the crisis, agreed. But we wanted to keep the salaries the same so that our people are motivated to give great service. One way to do that is to fire everybody we have to in order to keep core employees at the same wage. But there was also another way. Instead of lowering salaries, we saved with other concessions. We cut down on the vacation formula and made small reductions in benefits—*and kept the salaries the same.* We gave employees a choice, and they opted to keep their salaries stable.

We also doubled our training programs while many other hotels have stopped them. We also take our employees to the Dead Sea for a reward for good service, which they greatly appreciate. The employee satisfaction rating of this hotel has gone to the highest rating ever.

Q: Has your ability to plan for the long term been affected by the crisis?

Fortis: It's very difficult to plan long term because our guests are not planning long term. We don't have the backlog of reservations to respond to with planning. Everything is a last-minute decision.

Q: If the Hilton people were to ask you to give a speech to all the chain managers, worldwide, about coping with crisis, what would be your main theme?

Fortis: I suppose I would tell them, "Don't let the market dictate who you are." We are doing what is good for us, even though it's against the trend of cut, reduce, cut, reduce. The Waldorf-Astoria should not react in the same way as another, quite different hotel. You can adapt, sure, but only in context of your position in the market long term. This crisis, however long, will pass. And when it does, we are already prepared for the day after, because we haven't changed our product.

■ ■ ■

NOT LETTING THE MARKET DICTATE

Crisis management is, in some sense, the art of fighting fire with fire. There is a sudden, unwelcome change to the status quo, and the manager implements sudden changes within the organization in response—which are also unwelcome since they are sharp deviations from established routine. But everybody within the company understands there has been an emergency, and that you simply cannot continue as if nothing had taken place. After my interview with Ronnie Fortis, I got the distinct impression that some managers can successfully do just that—nothing.

What is it about change that seems to generate a mandate for like response? The momentum seems to gather all before it, lifting managers and executives to the conclusion that everything the company has been doing for years, or decades, is no longer appropriate to the new "paradigm." That change must be *responded to* is a modern axiom—and one, incidentally, that Madison Avenue has always played on as it beats the drum for a new wave of alleged demand for a "revolutionary" product or service. Even in a peaceful economy, grave business consultants advise their clients to keep pace with the ever-mutating forces of the competition. *Not* to change, we are advised, will lead to obsolescence or irrelevance. Since the very ability to react quickly is associated with youth, many CEOs and senior executives, no longer comfortable with appearing sage, dye their hair and adopt the jargon of the generation they should be mentoring instead of pandering to. In an age when dynamic business leaders build reputations for creativity and for "out of the box" solutions to "unprecedented" responses, the general manager—who, in effect, does nothing different—is not likely to appear on the glossy covers of the business magazines.

This is not to suggest that the intifada is anything less than a mortal threat to the Israeli economy, in general, and to the tourist industry in particular—or that the general managers previously interviewed have not literally saved their hotels through their ability to adapt brilliantly to the situation. But it is interesting that not all GMs felt similarly obligated to stage an organizational "shaking off" of their own in response to the terrorist crisis. And I think this has to do with one's position in the marketplace. In the words of Ronnie Fortis, "The Waldorf-Astoria should not react in the same way as another, quite different hotel." While it may appear risk averse, the refusal to change—while all of one's associates are staking their careers on truly revolutionary departures from the industry standard—may be the biggest risk of all. Should the illustrious Hilton Tel Aviv fail during the crisis, Ronnie Fortis would certainly be vulnerable to criticism that he did not sufficiently adapt to the emergency. On the other hand, when the crisis passes, the hotel will not have to reverse course to recapture its former grandeur or loyal clientele. In the meantime, there is something comforting about an establishment that, while not denying the emergency, refuses to accommodate it. Ronnie did not even acknowledge the duty of a general manager to rush about reassuring hotel guests after a terrorist attack. Yet the spectacle of that older man going about his business, unaffected, unafraid, and unimpressed with the enemy that is trying to instill fear throughout his country must be comforting in itself. It remains to be seen if the Hilton Tel Aviv can ride out the intifada without major concessions to the resulting economic depression—though, for the past four years of the terrorist crisis, it has apparently refrained from making the operational changes necessary to the profitability of many of its competitors. Depending on one's place in the market, this can be an inspirational story.

CHAPTER THREE

Checklist for Managing a Business Under Fire

- ❑ Cooperate with your competitors during a crisis.
- ❑ Be aware of the positive, unintended consequences of terror.
- ❑ Make your workplace a sanctuary.
- ❑ Assume a leadership role in the community.
- ❑ Remember that customer support may be lacking during a crisis.
- ❑ Say "No" to class-action lawsuits.
- ❑ Instill the Big Picture.
- ❑ Don't let the crisis "momentum" affect your position in the marketplace.

CHAPTER FOUR

Eleven Months' Annual Leave

■ ■ ■

"There are days, when tensions are particularly high, when I call my managers and ask them to bring their guns."

—*BARUCH PELED, MANAGING DIRECTOR, MANGO DSP*

ONE OF THE MOST STRIKING DIFFERENCES BETWEEN AN Israeli and an American company is the across-the-board, shared experience of military service. Although it is not uncommon for an American organization to have in its employ a small number of veterans and active reservists, virtually *everyone* in the Israeli company, male and female, is a veteran. All Israeli citizens, with the exception of a few religious sects and Arab-Israelis (who can volunteer), are required to enter the military at age 18. The men serve for three years of active service, the women for two. There is no choice in the matter and no postponing the entry date into the military to a more convenient time, such as after college. One can think of the system—which is modeled after the Swiss "total defense" system—as a draft, except that the term implies a temporary response to a grave national crisis. The Israeli military obligation is a way of life and probably will remain so for generations.

The subsequent active reserve requirement is forever—or so it must seem to an eighteen-year-old entering the service. Every Israeli male must serve in the reserves until age 45, if in a combat unit, or age 55, if in a support unit. Each man will spend a minimum of thirty days every year on active duty, which means, more often than not, thirty days in the West Bank or Gaza Strip, where being captured means death. This means that a very large proportion of Israel's businessmen are vetted combat veterans who are very likely to return to the areas of hostility, once a year, for decades. The term "citizen-soldier" hardly seems adequate; "soldier-citizen" more aptly describes the state of readiness each Israeli male must cultivate and maintain. I know if it were me, watching the calendar race towards my appointed thirty days of *combat,* I could worry about nothing else. Like a date for surgery looming on the horizon, it would color all of my thoughts. This is probably why so many Israelis consider their military active reserve obligation as "eleven months' annual leave" from active duty.

To appreciate the impact such a preponderance of military experience might have on a company, begin by imagining every person in your office, male and female—from the CEO to the mail room clerk—in the uniform of one of the branches of the armed forces. While the mental picture may provoke some humor (just imagine a few ill-fitting uniforms), it does suggest that a number of military virtues would be incorporated into the corporate culture—among them, teamwork, a can-do attitude, and an acceptance of hardship. You would also expect a much lower level of anxiety in a company composed of veterans who had fought and killed terrorists, who knew and exploited the weaknesses of terrorist groups, and who were absolutely not intimidated by threats of terror. Of all the economies in the world to attack, the enemies of Israel have chosen one that is populated with combat veterans.

This is not to say that Israelis take to the military obligation like ducks to water. Lest the reader be left with the impression of rank upon rank of obedient businessmen eager for orders to get back into combat, I should mention that there may be no other national character less suited to military service. I offer, by way of illustration, a comment by one of the interviewees. He had been in the United States to tour a Boeing plant and happened to witness a coffee break. Tens of thousands of workers suddenly ceased activities and quietly went about their fifteen-minute break, rising later in unison to resume the shift. He laughed and said, "Put 10,000 Israelis in the same room and there would be a free-for-all." Israelis, he explained, are entrepreneurial, impulsive, creative, and independent to the point of insubordination. It would be impossible, he felt, to harness such a naturally rebellious spirit in the way Boeing had managed as many Americans.

One of the most telling indications of this independent spirit is the national tradition of taking a year off, immediately after one's final day in active service, for the Israeli equivalent of a "walkabout," most commonly in India and Thailand. There are Hebrew road signs in these exotic locales, pointing the way for thousands of young Israeli men who have done their last push-up for a shouting drill instructor. The Israeli business community fully expects its future executives and managers to take this vacation in order to let off a little steam, and to eventually return, at age 22, and take on the responsibilities of adulthood.

Were one of these young men to go abroad for college, American professors might notice a marked contrast between a twenty-two-year-old Israeli and his American counterpart. Israeli men are beginning, as Americans are finishing, their academic studies. They are "old" freshmen. Many have led others into combat; all have apprenticed in one of the world's toughest militaries for the past three years, rather than frolicked on college campuses. The wild oats, in theory at least, have been sown in India; now is the time to begin one's education or career. In either case, the Israeli young man is likely to be a bit more mature than his American complement, although, perhaps, one step behind in his career path.

Interview with Baruch Peled,
Managing Director, Mango DSP

"Here we learn to make quick decisions, and we're not so afraid to fail."

Mango DSP is one of Israel's best-known high-tech companies. In business since 1996, it ranks eighth in the top fifty Israeli high-tech companies. Mango manufactures digital signal processors (DSPs), about which I know absolutely nothing, except that they are used in radar and medical imaging and in audio home electronics. Baruch Peled, managing director of Mango DSP, attempted to explain digital signal processing to me, in layman's terms. I listened very carefully, but there was evidently something in my expression that made him abandon the effort rather abruptly—and just when I was beginning to understand the thing about the ones and zeros. Baruch is in his midfifties and stands about five-feet-six. He has the hair of a lion, and a face that wrinkles into laugh lines during his frequent smiles. I think he has the kindest face I have ever seen.

Q: Have the high-tech companies with global customer bases been less affected by the intifada?

Peled: I don't know. But I know that *we* have been affected. The European market has dried up during the last three years. Europe has taken a stand on the issue, and it's against us. So we have gone to the U.S. and to the Far East.

And, because we are located in Jerusalem, it doesn't matter that we are a high-tech company; we are affected. Many of our employees live in the West Bank. Sometimes the roads are blocked. Sometimes they are shot at. We've responded by giving our people laptops so they can work at home. I'm a great believer in talking eye to eye, so sometimes communication is a problem. I'd prefer they were here at the office, but many days it's safer for them to work at home.

Q: Your employees are *shot at?*

Peled: Not every day, but sometimes, when tensions are high. One of my R&D managers has a choice of routes here to the office. He can take the safe route, which is a long hour-and-a-half drive each way, or he can take a shortcut, through the West Bank. You should see him. He wears a bulletproof vest and a motorcycle helmet. He's got a rifle in the back. We gave him a jeep with bulletproof windows.

Sometimes I have to go to the West Bank on business. I call my wife when I leave, and I call her when I get there.

Q: Besides having your employees in mortal danger, and losing market share in Europe, has the crisis had other effects?

Peled: [Laughing] Isn't that enough? Well, yes, our customers no longer come to Israel. Three years ago, many came. Today, we have to go to them.

Q: Have you taken measures to assure your customers, or investors, that Mango is just as reliable today as it was before?

Peled: Yes, we let our customers know that we have shipped production capability to the U.S. in case there is a bombing here. And we also do backups much more frequently.

Q: Is that simply to placate your customers, who may have inordinate fears fueled by the news media, or are you worried as well?

Peled: Ah, the news media! I stopped watching the news; it doesn't contribute to my health.

But are we worried? No, just prepared. We have management meetings, and we talk about what to do during an increase of terror. We have developed emergency plans to protect our people.

And there are days, when tensions are particularly high, when I call my managers and ask them to bring their guns. We are concerned, during an uprising, that they might come over here, and we've got to protect the business.

Q: Why not just close down shop on those days and tell everyone to stay home?

Peled: Because we are not going to give in to threats, or to terror—either here on the job or at home. I live in a village five miles from the West Bank. After every bombing in Jerusalem, my wife and I go for a walk in that area, just to show everybody—the terrorists and our neighbors alike—that nothing has changed, that life goes on as usual.

Q: Many of the people I interviewed who are in the tourist industry have a great deal of difficulty doing any long-term planning. Of course, their issue is the unpredictable nature of hotel occupancy. What about in your business—is it hard to make a plan and then implement it?

Peled: I am measured by growth, revenue, profit—these are the things my investors want. If I bring those numbers in from the American market and not from the European market as *planned,* then who cares if I stuck to my plan? I have to bring in results. As to how I get the results, I have to decide on a daily basis. Every quarter I update my investors and show them what I did.

And I encourage my managers to bring in results—any way they have to do it, as long as it is professional and ethical.

In the military, I learned to make decisions like this [snapping his fingers]. You get the best data you can and then decide, rather than waiting for more data. I've seen a lot of managers who hesitate. They're afraid to be wrong. Sometimes, though, you're going to be wrong. But if you're right 80 percent of the time, you're a valuable manager.

Q: What did you do in the military?

Peled: I spent twenty-six years in the air force. I was a lieutenant colonel, in system design. Now I'm back into the reserves, so I can occasionally work with my son. He's an officer in the tank corps. For my last tour, I took off my rank and drove my son's battalion commander around.

Q: What rank is a battalion commander?

Peled: A captain.

Q: You, a *colonel,* drove a captain around?

Peled: Sure, why not?

Q: You mentioned you have production capabilities in the United States, just in case of an emergency. If you had to manage a subsidiary in America, what would you try to cultivate in your American managers and employees?

Peled: Well, again, I go back to decision making. Here we learn to make quick decisions, and we're not so afraid to fail. It's better to make a decision and fail than to habitually wait until you are absolutely, positively, unequivocally sure, because by then the opportunity has passed you by. So I would encourage flexibility of mind, just as it has been encouraged in me. I would try to get my people to shorten the decision-making process.

■ ■ ■

THE WARRIOR MENTALITY

The mental picture of Baruch Peled's R&D manager speeding to work through no-man's-land, in a fortified jeep, wearing a bullet-proof vest, is both colorful and absolutely terrifying. Although it was no doubt kind of Baruch to provide his manager with a bullet-proof jeep, the need for such an unusual "perk" is outrageous. Not only must the adventurous R&D manager be prepared for a category of road rage beyond the comprehension of the average American commuter, but Baruch himself, as the managing director, must be very uneasy whenever the armored jeep is late in arriving. How many CEOs, whose corporate policies wisely forbid firearms on the premises for fear of workplace violence, can relate to Baruch's occasional phone call to his managers asking them to *bring* their guns to work? Clearly, some businesses in Israel operate under conditions akin to those encountered by the very first commercial outposts in the American Wild West.

One associates certain industries with a distinctive breed of employees. Oil-drilling platforms, high-rise construction sites, and Alaskan fishing boats are often worked by two-fisted, rough-and-ready types who scoff at danger. But Mango DSP manufactures processing chips; its employees are computer nerds! As this interview unfolded, I thought to myself that the business case for compulsory military service in Israel had just been made. It would be impossible to go to work every day at Mango DSP without a survivalist's attitude. That most, if not all, of Mango's employees are soldier-citizens is very relevant indeed. It would be difficult to imagine somebody without military training, and without the requirement to be "ready" eleven months out of the year, coping with that kind of daily stress. Not only do Mango's employees have a warrior mentality; they have a *wartime* mentality. It is a pity such a frame of mind is necessary, but their military training certainly has value during the terrorist-inspired crisis.

THE IMPORTANCE OF BUSINESS AS USUAL

The ritual "walk in the park" that Baruch and his wife made in the aftermath of a terrorist attack struck me as a gesture within the grasp of every citizen. It seemed such a simple act of subdued defiance, taken on one's own initiative. This is not something that Baruch organizes among his neighbors. In fact, a collective walk in the park would defeat his intention of showing the terrorists that "nothing has changed." Instead, it would be a rally, which *is* a change of normal routine. The identical determination to continue lifelong routines without interruption applies to his business as well. He knows how gratifying it would be for the terrorists if their very threats of violence led to the shutting down of Israeli businesses. It must be terribly frustrating for the terrorists to see that their best efforts have no appreciable effect on the rhythms of Israeli society. What "progress" resulting from their campaigns to make life unbearable for the average Israeli citizen can be noted when people like Baruch Peled maddeningly continue to stroll through the park as if the bus hadn't been bombed, as if the café were still intact?

Baruch's insistence upon maintaining normal routines, at home and at work, requires both courage and discipline. It requires courage because the terrorists could be watching, and discipline because of the personal outrage that must be stifled, so as not to entertain the terrorists. But continuing "business as usual" does not mean denial. Israeli executives and managers do not pretend nothing has happened; they just insist that nothing will change. Random acts of murder must, of course, be acknowledged so that the victims of terror receive the moral support they are entitled to expect. But the slightest sign of an altered Israeli business community would give hope to the terrorists, while also raising the concerns of one's employees, customers, investors, and prospective visitors. Israeli defiance, then, is akin to the underground resistance that thwarted the Nazi occupation of much of Europe. Behind a smiling, open demeanor, shopkeepers clandestinely fought the Nazis; any change in normal routine would have caught the eye of the invader. In a way, this is how the Israeli business community deals with the terrorist campaign against unarmed men, women, and children: The companies carry on, "unaffected." Israeli businesspeople know that their job is to compete in the marketplace just as vigorously as before. It's just that now, business "success" is doubly sweet: The new contract has been won, and the terrorists have been denied.

CULTIVATING "FLEXIBILITY OF MIND"

Baruch's penchant for more rapid decision making can certainly be cultivated. After all, it was cultivated in him during his military career. Certainly, there are workshops and seminars galore that put attendees through a "mini boot camp" of group and individual exercises designed to increase spontaneity and creative thinking. But once the workshop is over and the employee returns to the reality of her organization, the inhibiting fears of exposure also return. Rapid decision making has less to do with information-processing techniques and much more to do with one's comfort level with the tolerance of management. Would Baruch's 80-20 rule fly in corporate America? Certainly a manager who was "wrong" 20 percent of the time would find his career with the company in jeopardy. That's why so many managers are more concerned with escaping the consequences of failure than leading their teams to success.

That his 80-20 standard for a successful manager comes from the Israeli Air Force should not be a surprise. The "strict and inflexible" military is much more tolerant of mistakes than most business organizations. In battle, the windows of opportunity can be very narrow. To complicate matters, incoming information can be contradictory and biased by personality. There is often little to go on and scant time to make a command decision upon which lives may depend. Because of the fluidity of the battlefield situation, the moment must be seized. That is why the military expects its officers to *act* rather than reflect, like Hamlet, over the pros and cons of a proposed course of action. When evaluating an officer, the high command is less concerned with the results of his actions and more interested in the timeliness of the orders given. The military does not expect omniscience. As long as the officer made the best of the situation and acted aggressively, "senior management" is much more understanding of a failure to achieve the desired objective than the Hollywood stereotypes would have us believe. Generals know from firsthand experience that battlefield conditions can change in the blink of an eye and that the prerequisites of a successful outcome—such as the arrival of key logistical support, the weather holding up as predicted, and other elements in the coordinated attack coming into play as planned—are out of the field officer's control.

Military commanders take the long view. With few exceptions, their love and loyalty to the organizations they serve inspire decisions based on the future benefits to the organization, rather than on their individual careers. To the military's credit, senior commanders, like judges, are somewhat insulated from the hue and cry of the political apparatus. There is no real equivalent of a board of directors asking a CEO, "What have you done for me lately?" This long-term, comparatively philosophical view makes allowances for failure. Every general or admiral will confess to having been a bumbling, "shavetail" junior officer who had the very good fortune of being mentored by the older hands in the organization. His counterpart in the business world, however, may not be able to look back on such a nurturing corporate culture. Senior managers in corporate America may be less tolerant of mistakes because they are under pressure to get to the bottom of a wayward business decision—not so much to find out what went wrong, but to discover "who" was responsible. The top-down search for accountability does not go unnoticed. Managers throughout the rank and file think in terms of their own potential defense, should one of their decisions go awry. Baruch Peled would probably contend these managers are too risk averse, too deliberative, too self-protective to seize a business opportunity as it flashes momentarily in front of their eyes. His advice to shorten the decision-making process is well taken, but in order for that flexibility to take hold, there must be a concomitant flexibility on the part of the owners and shareholders, whose insistence on immediate returns, quarter to quarter, creates a free agent, cover-your-assets frame of mind.

▪ ▪ ▪

Interview with Barry Spielman, Director of Corporate Marketing, Gilat Satellite Networks

"I go into a dark mood. I am filled with rage and want to be alone. Work becomes a sanctuary for me."

Gilat Satellite is one of the world's leading providers of satellite-based communications systems. Based outside of Tel Aviv, the company has subsidiaries all over the world. Gilat has, in fact, set up the satellite network for about 12,000 United States Postal Service offices across America. The New York office, unfortunately, was not one of them; its non-satellite-based communications system went down, along with just about everything else, in the first hours of the attack on September 11, 2001. Other offices, however, were able to bring Gilat's technology to New York, point it at the satellite, and reestablish communications very quickly.

I was eager to meet Barry Spielman, director of corporate marketing, because we had corresponded via e-mail. Perhaps because he was born in New York, he was one of the few Israeli executives to express a willingness to talk to an outsider like me about the terrorist problem. Most of the other interviewees in this book would do so only after the Ministry of Industry and Trade vouched for my character and credentials. I met Barry in one of Gilat's conference rooms. We were joined by two of his associates. Shire (pronounced "Shira") is an American from Arizona who has lived in Israel the past nine years. Monique is from Israel but travels to New York frequently to visit family. Both women are in their late twenties and easy on the eyes. Barry is in his forties, physically fit, and an interviewer's dream—articulate and ready to answer. The women, for the most part, were content to let him take the lead.

Q: You mentioned in one of your e-mails that, because of the global customer base, Gilat Satellite has not been directly affected by the terror of the last four years. But I would imagine there are indirect effects of the intifada that pose managerial challenges.

Spielman: Yes, our problems stemmed from the high-tech crisis; the intifada was the icing on the cake. Hundreds were fired, and there have been no salary increases in years. And the crisis affects us just like any other business with employees that have to get to work. Terror "alerts" can be daily events with road closings, detours, car inspections, traffic jams that take hours out of the workday. I mean this happens *all the time.* In some ways, a terror alert can be just as disruptive to a society as an actual attack.

And, as to the actual terrorist attacks: I know five people who have been killed in bus bombings. It makes me realize they are targeting all of us; the fact that I haven't been directly affected is pure luck.

We had a bombing four blocks from this facility. A grandmother and her granddaughter were killed at an ice cream parlor. The mother lived. But who did CNN interview? The mother of the suicide bomber. There was such an outcry on the part of the Israeli population that CNN executives flew out here to save the market.

Shire: I was driving home and saw the traffic jams, the ambulances. You get to know the signs. I knew immediately there had been another suicide bombing. Then I turned on the news and heard the details.

Q: How do you deal with a workforce that shows up the next day, bringing all kinds of emotional reactions to the job?

Spielman: Speaking for myself, when something like this happens, I go into a dark mood. I am filled with rage and want to be alone. My wife and kids pay the price, but I can't help it. Work becomes a sanctuary for me; it's a place to put my mind on something else. Others feel this way, too. So, it's not as bad as you might think, at least at your place of work.

Q: Do you ever lose good managers because they're tired of bringing up their families with so much violence going on?

Monique: You've raised an awkward question. Shira and I are both wrestling with this right now.

Q: Well, then, there is a managerial challenge to keep you two in the company. Have you been approached from the highest level and told how much your efforts are appreciated?

Monique: There is nothing the company could say, or do, to keep me. If I decide to go, then I'll go.

Shire: Yes, it's not a matter of a pep talk from upper management.

Spielman: But we have not lost managers due to the terror. And I hope we don't lose these two. Most Israelis have become accustomed to the attacks, which in itself is kind of sad, I suppose. But we're used to crisis in this country. Just a few months ago, during the Iraqi War, we had every reason to expect missiles to fall on us—just like during the Gulf War when forty missiles hit us. So we were ready.

Monique: We had different sealed rooms, here at this facility, in case there was a chemical attack. Each room had a port-a-potty and water and rations. A roster on the front door had the names of those assigned to each room. The government issued an order for everyone to carry a gas mask with them at all times.

Spielman: [Laughing] During the first Gulf War, there was a coincidental immigration into Israel of hundreds of thousands of Russian Jews. They were met at the airport and were told, "Welcome to Israel. Here's your gas mask."

Q: So, then, do you run drills in these emergency shelters?

Monique: Yes. Somebody is assigned to make sure everybody is in their particular room. Then we all put on the gas masks and stay there until the drill is over.

Spielman: We're all pretty adept at putting on gas masks. You have to remember, during the Gulf War, we did forty drills for *real.*

That was a time when the Israeli housewife was the true hero. We men were deployed in the field, in defensive positions. The wives were the ones alone in the home, with sealed rooms for the families.

During the first weeks of the Gulf War, the missiles were falling in Tel Aviv. Some people left Tel Aviv to visit friends in the surrounding areas. But many residents argued that the people should stay and not show fear. [Laughing] Nothing happens here without a controversy.

I was in the army and I was driving with my commander to a nearby town. Halfway there, the air raid sirens go off. What you're supposed to do is pull off the road and put on your mask. We were good army types, so that's what we did. Ninety percent of the cars just drove by, ignoring the order. We both sat in the car, wearing our gas masks, feeling stupid. Finally, my commander says, "The hell with this," and she starts to drive with her mask on. Have you ever worn a gas mask? You can hardly see out of those things. So the car begins to swerve a bit. I told her, "Let's take these things off and take our chances, because you're not driving me wearing a gas mask."

Q: How long were you in the army?

Spielman: I joined when I first moved here, twenty years ago, and rose to the rank of major, which isn't bad for an American kid from New York.

Q: Are society's reactions to a soldier being killed in an act of terror different from when a civilian is killed by a similar act?

Spielman: Definitely. Our soldiers are being killed all the time, but there is less of an outcry. When someone decides to blow himself up in the Maxim restaurant, after purposely maneuvering to be near a baby carriage, society is horrified. But just a short time later, somebody slipped into a military range and, at point-blank range, put a bullet in the heads of two sleeping women. But they were part of the military, so somehow our society can deal with it better. But I can't.

Speaking about soldiers and civilians, don't forget that the heroes here are very often civilians. It happens all the time: an armed citizen running down a terrorist, or a passenger throwing a suicide bomber off the bus.

Q: Overall, what has been the most noticeable effect of the intifada on your business these last three years?

Spielman: The lack of visitors. Our customers used to come here all the time.

Monique: Sometimes even your own family won't come; they're too afraid. If that can happen on a personal level, you can bet it will happen on a business level.

Q: You've all had plenty of experience in America. How do you think Americans would react if, God forbid, this kind of terror campaign was launched against them?

Spielman: An American friend told me that if a bomb goes off in a theater in the United States, then nobody will go to the theater. I hope my friend is wrong. Because you must not change your way of life. The Israeli population has more experience with this thing than any other country in the world. If we have a soccer game scheduled and there is a terrorist event right before that game, the game begins on time. We won't change the way we live.

DRILLING FOR TERROR ATTACKS

After the interview, I was taken to one of the sealed rooms. On the front door hung a clipboard that listed about twenty names. Inside, it was difficult to imagine how twenty adults would be able to fit, unless they were all standing. A portable toilet was enclosed with a shower curtain. On the shelves were enough provisions to last, I assumed, the duration of a chemical attack. I tried to imagine the exercise: twenty friends from the office, all crammed in this small room, all wearing gas masks. Certainly the first drill against a possible chemical attack would have its share of gallows humor, as everyone looked at each other through the goggles of the gas masks. Voices would be muffled and difficult to identify. There would, no doubt, be "monster" imitations by the office prankster; two employees may attempt a platonic kiss, mask to mask; and an exasperated monitor might laugh at his own attempts at keeping order.

But, sooner or later, the outrageous implications for the practical necessity of such a drill would sink in. A ruthless enemy may very likely attack with poison gas—perhaps a gas similar to the mixtures used to kill one's grandparents in the concentration camps or, more recently, to kill thousands of Kurds in their villages, or to attack subway commuters in Tokyo. During an actual attack, the thoughts of Gilat's employees would be of their families and how they were faring in similar rooms at the schools, at community shelters, and at home. The cell phones would be on, all over the nation, as family members reassured one another. Standing in that room, I could feel some of the anxiety, and the sense of helpless isolation, one might feel during the real thing.

My only reference point in the American workplace was the "fire drill," mandated by the insurance companies, in which we all, groaning in protest, have to go through the motions of responding to an *accidental* emergency. None of us ever consider ourselves the potential target of an intentional attack; we are "drilling" because of the remote possibility that the janitor's coffeepot might spark a fire in the basement of the building. While it is true that, since 9/11, fire drills in high-rise office buildings have taken on a new meaning, the goal is to get everybody out of the building into the fresh air. In Gilat's scenario, that very air would be deadly; employees would be huddled in claustrophobic rooms, presumably for hours, until the "all clear" signal were sounded. It seemed incredible to me that in the twenty-first century such precautions were necessary.

Suddenly I realized Israel was, by virtue of its proximity to its neighbors, oddly lucky. A nuclear or biological attack may actually be less likely because of the uncontrollable consequences. Even dedicated terrorists might not relish the thought of a smallpox epidemic taking place one zip code away. America, however, separated from its enemies by the oceans, might be a more likely candidate for truly horrendous, systemic weapons of mass destruction.

If ever a company wanted a "team-building exercise," surely this was it. There would be absolutely no need for pep talks from the managers; the sealed-room drill would sufficiently hammer home the message to Gilat's employees that they must function together during a terrorist attack if they want to survive. Reminding Israeli employees that they live in extraordinary times is not the issue; getting all of them to stick through the crisis, however, is definitely a managerial challenge, and a responsibility.

I didn't quite believe Monique and Shire when they said there was nothing the company could do to persuade them to stay, should they decide to leave. I gathered, rather, that such an effort had not been made from senior management, and that *that* could have been part of the problem. Certainly any young mother who drives by a demolished ice cream parlor would have second thoughts about living in an environment where a grandmother, mother, and child had been intentionally targeted, out of all the people in the mall, for murder. Remaining in such an environment is a lot to ask of a mother, but the CEO must ask it. Business leaders cannot allow their valued employees to dwell on leaving the company without first letting them know how much they are needed. If talented people do ultimately leave, senior management has the consolation of having done its best, on a very personal level, to express its appreciation. Employees who believe the organization would be wounded by their leaving will feel somewhat obligated to remain. Although perhaps not the decisive factor, loyalty to an organization will be one of the *deciding* factors. Combined with other considerations, such as office friendships, a clear career path, and the solicitous support of middle management, it may swing the individual over. Not to make such an outreach is an opportunity lost on the part of the company executives.

■ ■ ■

The Dolphinarium Bombing: Interview with David Cohen and Zeev Keren, David Intercontinental Hotel

"You think you've seen it all. We've all been in the military and have seen horrible things, but this was the worst."

I had the good fortune to stay in the David Intercontinental Hotel for two weeks, which gave me a chance to have several conversations with General Manager David Cohen and his assistant and mentor, Zeev Keren. Cohen is the younger of the two, close to forty, tall and strong. Keren is in his midfifties, broad shouldered, and substantial. I mention their physical size because it may have been of some comfort to their very nervous guests after the horrific suicide bombing at the Dolphinarium, across the street, in June 2002. The Dolphinarium was a discothèque, so named because it was adjacent to a large dolphin aquarium. On that warm summer night, a suicide bomber insinuated himself into the long line of teenagers, patiently waiting to be passed through by the security guard at the door. Waiting until he was surrounded by the maximum number of Israelis—most of them new émigrés from Russia—the bomber suddenly detonated himself. The resulting carnage was unimaginable. Twenty-eight young people were killed outright, scores were wounded, some for life. The Dolphinarium is still out of business, although, as I understand it, for reasons other than the terror attack. A year and a half after the bombing, I walked the short distance from the hotel to the Dolphinarium and peeked through the painted glass doors into the barren lobby. Someone had placed a bouquet of flowers, now a week or so old, on the doorstep. Several stubby candles had burned down to the wick.

The bombing had a chilling effect on the business of nearly all of the hotels in Tel Aviv, none closer than the David Intercontinental. What follows is a fascinating study of personal leadership under the most trying circumstances a hotel manager may encounter in a career.

Q: Can we start off with the Dolphinarium? That had to be one of your greatest challenges.

Cohen: My wife and I were out to dinner. I got a call that there had been an explosion *inside* the hotel—that's how strong the blast was. I raced over here and saw the police cars just arriving. So I got out to help. . . . It was shocking. You think you've seen it all. We've all been in the military and have seen horrible things, but this was the worst. Twenty-eight teenagers—*children* to me—blown apart.

Within minutes of the bombing, some of our guests got dressed and went to the reception desk and said, "Get me out of here, on *any* plane; I don't care where it's going."

Q: You didn't try to calm their fears and persuade them to stay?

Cohen: I didn't try to persuade anyone to stay; in fact, we launched into helping them leave as soon as possible. Less than a dozen guests left. The guests from companies abroad waited for directions. They were told by their headquarters to stay in the hotel for a couple of days. We cleared the lines for them to phone their families. We upgraded their services, so they could sit in the executive lounge on the twenty-fourth floor and relax. We, too, would go up there and talk with them.

One big American company had been here for months. Five Americans had just finished dinner at a restaurant next door to the Dolphinarium. They were walking back to the hotel when the explosion sounded. We all went into the cigar bar here and had drinks and talked. It was two in the morning.

My managers and I finally went to sleep at 4:00 A.M. and woke at 7:00 A.M., to be in the breakfast room, so we could talk to our guests. They saw that the managers weren't hiding in their offices but making themselves available. It was just as important for our staff to see that as well.

Q: I'll bet your guests were relieved to see you and Zeev all around the hotel.

Cohen: I think so. I even joked to the American group: "If something happens, we go together." But, yes, Zeev and I were everywhere. We slept in the hotel and constantly made the rounds. As a hotel manager, you're onstage all the time.

In the Israeli military, officers are trained to say "Follow me," versus "Go ahead." So that's what we did.

Q: Did the guests hold up pretty well?

Keren: Many were airline crews from Continental and other airlines, so they're a tough bunch. They have stayed here for years, and we've always been very frank with them about the situation here. During the Gulf War, we took the airline crews to see our shelters, in case of chemical attack, and showed them the gas masks. We had a shelter on each floor, so nobody would have to run down to the basement.

But we always remind ourselves that, although *we* may be used to the problems here, our guests are not. So we want to be here to reassure them. Whenever the police get intelligence that something bad might happen, we discreetly move into the hotel.

We don't hide the security, here, like they do in America. You want the guests to see the measures taken.

Cohen: Yes, the guests were splendid. They appreciated our honesty; but, you know, the honest truth was, they were safe in the hotel. This is a modern hotel and designed so that it is easy to seal. In fact, President Clinton once stayed here because the FBI and Secret Service decided this was about the easiest hotel to secure in Tel Aviv.

Q: Did the newness of the hotel give you any advantage in coping with the intifada?

Cohen: Perhaps. Because our whole operation was new, maybe we could experiment more. When the terrorism began in October of 2000, we anticipated the worst and reacted accordingly. We cut our staff by more than half within three weeks. We believed our occupancies would drop to 15 to 20 percent. We pretty much pioneered outsourcing the major departments within the hotel. At the time, other hotels told us it couldn't be done; now they are outsourcing as well.

That April, we finished the month averaging 17 percent occupancy, with $1,000 profit! That we made a profit at all was unthinkable at that level of occupancy. People in our industry realized we had just rewritten the textbook on how to run a hotel.

Q: With half the staff fired, were the survivors walking on eggshells?

Cohen: They were nervous. But we told them the truth: "We've chosen you out of the crop to lead this hotel through the crisis. If we drop to 15 percent occupancy, this team will have to be narrowed down, so let's do all we can to not lose occupancy, and to increase it."

I was very reluctant to fire the junior managers because they had been apprenticing here, and they were our future. So we transferred five managers overseas to other hotels. In some cases, they took a subordinate role there because the management positions were already filled. We had one lady, for example, who went to the Churchill [Hotel] in London as a reservations agent, although here she was a reservations manager. The Churchill told us they could only pay her half what she was earning here, so we said we will pay the other half. This crisis will not last forever, and we want those managers back.

The one department that we didn't reduce was sales. While most hotels have pulled back on their sales force, we have recruited. In fact, we have recruited some of the salespeople let go from our competition. There is business out there. That is the one department that has grown in this hotel during the crisis.

Q: You mentioned to me earlier that you, too, went to London.

Cohen: We moved to London for a year and a half. The first time we went to a mall, my daughter tugged on my sleeve, wanting to know why there were no guards with guns checking our bags.

Q: Was your daughter afraid to come back?

Cohen: Like all kids here, she knows what's going on. The kids all talk. A few weeks ago, she came home from school shaking all over. She said, "Daddy there was a terrorist waiting outside in a green car, waiting to blow us up." So I said, "Let's go for a drive." As we headed for the school, I asked her what the terrorist was wearing. She answered emphatically, "A green shirt." I asked what color shoes he had on, and she answered, "Brown." "But how could you see his shoes," I asked her, "if he was sitting in the car?"

So, bit by bit, she began to realize this image was at least in part built up in her imagination. But there's enough of the real thing here to make their imaginations run wild.

We had dinner together in a café just as we returned from London. Suddenly there was a terrific explosion. I ran outside to see the fire trucks arriving. It was not what I thought, thankfully—a gas line had exploded in an empty building. But my daughter was crying and shivering. It's scary for kids. And for us, too.

Q: What did you do in the military?

Keren: David was an officer in the navy, and I was in artillery.

Q: Does your military experience help you in this crisis, with planning, for example?

Cohen: Planning in this business, at this point in time, is a paper exercise.

Q: But don't your owners expect a business plan, with the pie charts, the predicted margins?

Cohen: Our investor paid $140 million for this hotel and expects to see a return. There are a lot of indicators that will tell him if we are ahead or behind the market. If he has faith in his management team, and sees that they are doing all they can, he will accept the numbers, whatever they are, *as long as they're 2 or 3 percent ahead of the competition.*

If all the other hotels are at 35 percent occupancy and your owner demands 65 percent, there is a hidden agenda; you are at the wrong place at the wrong time.

So our plan is this: If you have an opportunity for *today*, do everything to get it. If you have an opportunity for six months from now, sure, you work hard to get it, but you know that something could happen and you could lose it.

Q: If, as you say, Israeli hotel managers have rewritten the books about hotel operations, will the major chains start transferring GMs from Tel

Aviv and Jerusalem to hotels abroad, to institute some of the changes you've made here?

Cohen: [Laughing] Hotel chains are very dominant about their policies worldwide. We are pretty much left alone here to manage in this unique situation. I'm not sure they want a bunch of mavericks like us managing all of the hotels in the world. If you were to put Israelis in the hotel chains in America, for example, things would fall apart very soon—because everyone is smarter than the other, everyone knows better, everyone wants to be prime minister.

■ ■ ■

LEADING IN THE AFTERMATH OF A TERRORIST ATTACK

As noted in previous interviews, hotels must be able to offer peace and quiet to their customers. Although guests may go out in search of the nightlife, they expect to sleep in soundless suites afterward. Peace and quiet is what they pay for. The guests at the David Intercontinental, and at any Tel Aviv or Jerusalem hotel in the summer of 2002, were well aware of the tensions within Israel; the intifada had, after all, been going on for a year and a half. They may not have been surprised to read about a bus bombing in the morning papers, but an explosion just across the street, so powerful that it shook them out of their beds, came as a terrifying shock. It also presented a challenge to every employee in the hotel.

True to his solicitous nature, David Cohen's first response was to help the dozen or so understandably panicked guests who wanted to leave. One would think that gesture, alone, calmed the fears of the other guests, who could readily see that there was an avenue of escape, should they elect to take it. They were not "trapped" in the hotel. The avenue of escape being open, escaping could be postponed. What David and Zeev did, then, was right out of the officer candidate textbooks: They shared the risk. There is nothing more comforting to a customer than a vendor who throws his lot in with the success of a given venture, come what may. The same applies to the hotel staff, when they see their manager associate his own fate with their fate. The ubiquitous presence of both men—working on three hours of sleep—must have been an inspiration to both guests and employees. Imagine the anxiety that would have been provoked by their inexplicable absence—if, for example, they had spent the night at home with their families, as is the norm, and had delegated the oversight of the hotel to the night manager.

By providing a complimentary sanctuary for all of the guests, David Cohen very subtly discouraged the isolation that, in times of crisis, can contribute to panic. It is a good bet that before the bombing many of the guests in the twenty-fourth floor lounge had not met each other. They were there on business; statistically, few pure tourists flew to Israel in 2002. With busy schedules all, it would have been unlikely that flight crews, software engineers, academicians, and manufacturers' reps had interacted with each other. Suddenly, after the bombing and during the lockdown of the hotel, these strangers were thrown together, thanks to the benign manipulation of the hotel's general manager. The relief of having others to talk to who were not "locals" inured to nightclub bombings must have been immense.

It is axiomatic that in the hotel industry, one has to smile—managers, receptionists, waiters, and housekeepers alike. But there are smiles, and there are smiles. In the immediate aftermath of a bloody massacre, David and Zeev were probably two rather serious hotel managers; any kind of happy-face pretense would have been so out of place as to inspire fear in the guests. Even assurances of absolute safety could not be offered with credibility. What could be shared, though, were the security measures taken. But, certainly, smiles of commiseration would have been appropriate as both men made the rounds throughout the hotel. Even a little gallows humor, with a guest robust enough to appreciate it, would lessen the tension. This is why David's joke, "If something happens, we go together," was so telling. He was establishing a bond with the customer that may not be forgotten, while simultaneously demonstrating his own confidence in the outcome.

Through personal example, both managers led staff and guests through a very rattling experience. Their solid presence throughout the crisis turned what could have been an extremely negative association with the David Intercontinental Hotel into a warmer memory. Surely no guest who had been through the Dolphinarium bombing could have faulted the hotel, even on a subconscious level. On the contrary, the David Intercontinental may remain guests' first choice for the next visit, thanks to the leadership of David Cohen and Zeev Keren.

THINKING LIKE AN OWNER DURING THE CRISIS

David Cohen's efforts to secure opportunities abroad for his junior managers were not simply to befriend hardworking assistants; his primary concern was for the future of the hotel. That he took such an interest in these managers may not be notable in itself, until one remembers the context of his efforts. The intifada had provoked across-the-board draconian cost-cutting measures. Half of the employees had been let go; entire floors had been closed; the heat had been turned off. Every expense had to be justified. To subsidize 50 percent of the salaries of managers who would not be contributing to the bottom line of the David Intercontinental, and who, in fact, would be working for other hotels, was an extraordinary example of long-term thinking at a time when every hotel in Tel Aviv and Jerusalem was in survival mode. Not only was he thinking beyond the crisis; he may have been—depending upon the ages of the junior managers—thinking beyond his own tenure as general manager of the hotel. An employee who looks that far into the future, when the future of the tourist industry itself is in question, is thinking like an owner.

Now, either David Cohen takes a proprietary interest in his job by nature, or his sense of ownership has been cultivated by the actual owner. Since the former case cannot be replicated (short of cloning him), the latter is worthy of examination. How *does* an owner promote such a possessive attitude on the part of his employees? One way, clearly, is to make literal "owners" out of them all by awarding merit-based stock options. If the company is privately held, performance bonuses based on year-end margin would give every employee a stake in the profitability of the organization. Monetary reward does not entirely explain David's long-term view. He did, however, reveal a few working parameters specific to that hotel and unique to doing business in Israel during the current crisis. For one thing, the expectations of the owner are supremely realistic. The benchmark for success is *2 percent to 3 percent ahead of the competition.* The pressure to outperform the other four-star hotels in Tel Aviv is mandated, but the goal is fluid, as befits an industry in which the occupancy rate cannot be predicted. Imagine the effect of being saddled with the same goals as the other hotels in the worldwide chain that were assigned targets appropriate for a bustling tourist industry. The Israeli general manager would be beaten on the very first day of the fiscal year. By adjusting the David Intercontinental's goal for the unprecedented terrorist-inspired situation in Israel, the owner is giving him his moral support while making "success" possible.

The other interesting aspect of Cohen's situation as a GM in Israel is the lack of "hands-on management" from corporate headquarters. The David Intercontinental may be the only hotel in the worldwide chain in which the GM has so much authority—and with authority comes a sense of ownership. Nothing could be more ludicrous than receiving one's marching orders from a remote superior thousands of miles away who has no idea of the very unique challenges faced by an Israeli hotel manager. Sometimes the greatest vote of confidence is simply leaving a manager alone. And, left alone and in charge, how could Cohen not begin to think of the David Intercontinental as *his* hotel? To the degree he can pass that sense of pride along, others in the hotel will feel similarly about *their* departments.

The mentoring issue, however, has yet to be explained. What could prompt a general manager to think beyond his own tenure, other than a love for the organization? It certainly wasn't passion to keep the hotel afloat during the intifada that led to the decision to subsidize paychecks for off-site managers; his bottom line would have looked a lot better without this self-assumed burden. By sending his junior managers abroad, he was also taking the very real risk that they might "go native" and remain permanently at these "temporary" positions, in comparatively peaceful Europe, where hotel managers can advance their careers much more readily. His gesture, in that case, would not even have benefited the David Intercontinental, but the wider chain of hotels instead. Clearly, his regard for the organization, and for the owners, exceeds personal ambition.

A wise owner will not only reward deeds that contribute to the greater good of the organization, but quantify them as well. While "mentoring" does not show up on the pie charts documenting performance during the fiscal year, the sacrifice of one's time and energy for long-term results should be part of the expectations of upper management. And it should be measured in subjective evaluations—and then publicly celebrated, so that soon other managers in the company will be tripping over themselves to contribute to the bigger picture. In addition, just as managers are expected to mentor, the owner must be a mentor as well. All major "ownership" decisions—the kind that are often made behind closed doors, then revealed to senior and middle management at a later date—should include the input of top managers so that they begin to think in even larger images than their own future with the company. Someone like David Cohen, while no doubt focused on his livelihood, is the kind of manager who will earnestly try to leave the hotel, upon transfer or retirement, in better hands than his own. While much of that desire may come from his military training, it is a safe bet that his owner has taken some care to cultivate more than a sense of custody.

Interview with Michael Berman, CEO, Biomedicom

"Then, after the news reports of bus bombings and shootings, our investor pulled back."

Israel, during the 1990s, was known throughout the world's high-tech markets as the land of the start-up companies. Start-ups were the product of government-subsidized "seed" investments, and they were almost always to be found in the technology fields. The companies are characteristically youthful in terms of the number of years in existence, of course, but also in the age of their managers and the audacity of their business plans. Very many start-ups have been founded by military buddies, in the tradition of America's Flying Tigers freight airline begun after World War II. That the companies would predominately play in the high-tech market is fairly predictable since the Israel Defense Forces (IDF) is the most technologically advanced military in the world, and those leaving active duty return to the free enterprise system as experts in their field. The great frustration of many start-up companies is that they are relatively unhampered by the terrorist crisis, because of their global customer base, yet abandoned by investors, because of the investor's perceptions of life in Israel.

Biomedicom produces ultrasound imaging software that helps doctors see a virtual, three-dimensional model of the patient's inner workings on their computer screens. Imaging technology has revolutionized the medical field, and Biomedicom is in the forefront of the industry. Michael Berman is in his midfifties, tall, with an unruly shock of gray hair that rises into the air. He gives the impression of an athletic, well-nourished Einstein. He fought in the Yom Kippur War, as a platoon commander of an armored division, and has served two months a year in the reserves for two decades. That means, of course, he has been "on call" for state emergencies and has found himself in shooting situations more than once as a reservist on active duty. We were joined in the interview by one of the founders of the company, Professor Rachel Nechushtai. Youthful and energetic, she seemed the perfect match for Berman's vitality.

Q: How long has Biomedicom been in business?

Berman: We opened our doors in 1998—right before the crash of the high-tech market and the beginning of the intifada. Perfect timing, huh?

Q: That's pretty rough for a company without a lot of resources. Have the start-ups been disproportionately hurt by the events of the last few years?

Berman: Oh, yes. Start-ups in Israel are having a hard time; the global investors are shying away. Many companies are registering in the U.S. in order to raise the funds and defining their facility, here in Israel, as an R&D branch. My gut feeling is that nine out of ten start-ups are failing. This is not only bad for Israel, but for the world. The start-ups bring a lot of excitement and talent into the markets.

We have been affected, too. The intifada has hurt us in our ability to raise funds from investors or venture capital firms. I'll give you an example. We were expecting an $8 million infusion of funds. The commitment had been made; the contract was in place; we were counting on the money and had taken some actions accordingly. Then, after the news reports of bus bombings and shootings, our investor pulled back.

We were told by the VC in New York, "Maybe if you were in Tel Aviv . . . but Jerusalem is out of the question—too much terror." He advised us to change our structure. Instead of having a subsidiary in the U.S., he told us to reverse things and put our main company in America, making *us* the subsidiary.

Q: How important is it for a start-up to host visitors?

Berman: Very important. Before the intifada, customers and investors would come here all the time; so would the people who would certify us for all of the [Food and Drug Administration] requirements. But not now.

We had one gentleman who was supposed to come here for training. He was searched in Munich so thoroughly that he was frightened by the experience and decided not to fly. We had some Italians who were warned by all of their associates not to come here. But they had to—there were some things that simply had to be done here at our facilities. So, they were very frightened. Once they got here and looked around and saw how normal life was, they were no longer afraid.

Q: That has got to be so frustrating. Is there any way to combat the popular conceptions, often misconceptions, of Israel?

Berman: Well, I try, through phone calls, e-mails. But if the investors won't come here, I go there. Last year, I went abroad to raise money. I told the investors the crisis was not relevant to us because we have a global customer base. It's only relevant in the imaginations of the investors. No good. I came home with my pockets empty. Fortunately, we were finally able to find three private investors, all American.

Normal companies can raise somewhere around $40 million. We raised $7 million, then turned to the banks, which is an expensive way to fund. We are struggling, to be sure, because half of what we raised came as a credit line from the banks, so we are burdened with the interest.

Q: If you've lost investors, have you also lost talented staff members?

Berman: No, and in some ways, it's easier to find good people now because more people are available. It used to be, when I interviewed people, it was more like they were interviewing *me*, as they were trying to decide if this was the company they wanted to join.

There are a lot more freelancers available today. I can subcontract the task, without making a long-term commitment to an employee. And, whenever I need people, they're available.

Q: Just about everyone you interview, or hire, has had military experience. Does that come in handy during a terrorist-inspired crisis?

Berman: Yes, because of the maturity, and team-building experience. Leading by example is promoted very strongly in the IDF.

Q: Rachel, what about planning? Many of the businesspeople I have spoken with have difficulty planning because the future is so difficult to forecast.

Nechushtai: I'll tell you one of the reasons why there is no long-term planning: This is not a normal country; it's a country of nervous wrecks. Everybody is near the radio; every hour we have to hear the news—what terror attacks have been foiled, what ones happened.

It's also hard to plan long term when potential investors or strategic partners back out because of the situation here. The intifada gives some people a good excuse not to do business with an Israeli company. It's not the risk factor; it's our world image. We're pretty bad at public relations, you know.

Not only is the intifada a good excuse for investors to say, "No"; it's a good excuse for Israeli companies to give up and to say, "We tried, but the political situation defeated us."

Q: Incidentally, why are most of the executives I'm interviewing over here male? Are there a disproportionately small number of female executives in Israel?

Nechushtai: [Laughing] In some ways this reminds me of America. I taught life sciences for three years at UCLA. It was difficult to understand why only 17 percent of most faculties are female, when over 50 percent of my students are female, and generally smarter than the men. Same thing with Israel: It's hard to pinpoint why more women are not executives.

■ ■ ■

NOT LETTING THE CRISIS BECOME AN EXCUSE

There seemed to be an inherent contradiction in the failure rate of the start-ups, given their composition. If these emerging companies were typically managed by young, aggressive, former military buddies, why were, in the opinion of Michael Berman, nine out of ten failing? I reminded myself that more than force of will was required to succeed in business, and even on the battlefield. The best soldiers will eventually lose if they are not supported logistically—if, for example, fuel, ammunition, and spare parts are not supplied when desperately needed. The young men and women leaving the IDF for careers in free enterprise have been accustomed to receiving that support. While the Israeli Army is a very Spartan, "lean and mean" organization with few creature comforts, the tools for success are readily supplied. One hears no complaints in the press from exiting Israeli soldiers about a lack of material and moral support from the high command. In the business world, though, that support has not been forthcoming for the start-up companies, primarily because of the terrorist crisis, which has spooked the global investors. Many talented entrepreneurial Israelis must put their dreams of ownership on hold and go to work for the more established companies, which have the resources to endure the crisis.

Rachel Nechushtai raised an interesting possibility, however. The unprecedented situation in Israel could be a ready-made excuse for any businessperson in search of a reason for personal failure. This is not to suggest that citing the terrorist crisis as the reason for failure would be disingenuous. Investors *have* backed away; the tourists *have* been too frightened to visit; the ripple effect *has* put 10 percent of the workforce out of work; and this *is* the worst economic crisis in the nation's history. Blaming the economic environment in Israel for one's inability to succeed would be just as legitimate, and as poignant, as blaming the Crash of 1929 for the soup lines of the Depression Era. Yet, it would seem that few Israelis think in these terms—as evidenced by the number of ambitious Israelis who remain in country. Business analysts have never suggested there is a "brain drain" of talent seeking opportunities outside of Israel, such as the migration of professionals from England who sought better livelihoods in America in the 1960s.

If one takes the hotel industry as a more representative sample of the Israeli business "attitude" (start-up companies being more susceptible to *any* change in the market, including the collapse of the high-tech bubble before the intifada), there has been no surrender. Although it's been hardest hit by the terrorist crisis, there are just as many hotels today in Israel as there were before the bombings began. For the few hotels that have closed, new ones have been completed and have opened for business. Today's Israeli hotels may look a little different, with guards at the entrances and in the parking garages, and they may feel different, with more blankets on the bed and the heat turned off to save on operating expenses, but they doggedly remain in business.

While national pride and the natural reluctance of the civilized to capitulate to brute force no doubt contribute to the defiance on the part of the Israeli business community, military training must play a role. If virtually all of Israeli business professionals, male and female, are products of IDF—and if virtually all of the businessmen remain in a state of high alert in the active reserves—then there is a certain bias for victory within the business community. The lessons of three years of active duty, reinforced every single year for at least thirty days of more active duty *for virtually the entire span of one's business career,* are apt not to be forgotten. The military promotes a winning attitude even more than the corporation, which often compromises with the competitor and thinks in terms of win-win solutions. The military thinks instead in win-lose terms, and such a philosophy of life does not accept defeat graciously.

Every hotel manager I interviewed for this book had been challenged in ways that should have resulted in bankruptcy. Coincidentally, every manager had been a former military officer. None even hinted at the possibility of being run out of business by thugs, or of referencing the current economic crisis as the cause of a temporary shutdown of operations, or even as a cause for reducing the quality of service. Perhaps a similar defiance, under similar circumstances, could be found in a business community that is not populated with so many military veterans and active reservists. But, if so, the inspiration would have to come from *somewhere.* Business professionals, as a rule, prefer not to antagonize, not to take a stand, and not to cut themselves off from an avenue of escape. Without a core belief in their right to exist in a free market, even the most prominent business leaders may be susceptible to the persuasive arguments of terror.

■ ■ ■

Interview with Moshe Gaon, CEO, Baumann Ber Rivnay Saatchi & Saatchi

"Here, investors don't believe in the long-term plans; they believe in the manager."

Moshe Gaon runs one of the largest advertising agencies in the country. A former army commando, he is a combat veteran who, in his early forties, looks perfectly capable of crawling under barbed wire with a knife held between clenched jaws (which is how I always picture commandos). His offices are very stylish, as befits an advertising agency, with young attractive people running about, carrying sketches and glossy photographs. Instant "Israeli coffee" was served, and I wondered for a moment if I would become converted to the stuff before I returned to the United States. After a sip, the moment passed, and the answer was an unequivocal "No."

Q: I've interviewed quite a few people in the high-tech and tourist industries, but you're my first advertising firm. I would imagine the ripple effect of the terrorist crisis affects advertising in a big way.

Gaon: Yes, the first thing managers do, in whatever company, is to cut back on advertising during a recession. I've heard over the years so many executives say that the worst thing you can do during a recession is to cut on advertising. But, in reality, that's what they all do. Even if they don't specifically cut on advertising, they cut their budgets, meaning there is less to spend on advertising.

A lot of companies have closed, and there have been a lot of bankruptcies. Even the multinational companies are spending less.

And there is a fine point. Even companies that have the vision not to cut back on their budgets are *still* spending less on advertising—because now their smaller competitors no longer advertise, and they don't *have* to spend as much.

Q: Does that apply to your smaller competitors as well?

Gaon: Sure, because, overall, the economy is shrinking. The small competition is disappearing, and the big companies are increasing their share. But they are increasing their share in a decreasing market. Now what you have are the big companies—Procter & Gamble, Unilever, Nouveaux, and Strauss—competing against themselves.

Now, we're big, too, in the advertising market, so that's good because the big companies come to us. But our problem is just like theirs: We are "big" in a shrinking market. So, in order to increase our volume, we are organizing groups of agencies to work under us.

Q: Advertising is kind of like the tourist industry, in the sense that you always have to smile and express optimism for an upcoming campaign. Also you're promoting the good life with your ads—fun, excitement, vitality. Is that harder to do, today, when there is so much terror?

Gaon: Yes and no. Israelis have very short memories, and that's good for advertising people like myself. Give Israelis two or three days after a terror attack and they forget there ever was an attack. They bounce back. The streets are cleaned, the blood is washed away, and it's back to business as usual. It's sad to say, but this is true.

And that's the way Israelis can live in this country, because if you had a long memory, you'd never be able to live here.

Q: But, from a business perspective, isn't it true that those with a short memory are doomed to repeat the mistakes of the past?

Gaon: [Laughing] And we do! Israelis are the most "mistake repeatable" people in the world—except for the Palestinians, who repeat even more mistakes.

Q: Of the last four years, what period has been the worst for your business?

Gaon: In 2003, we had the worst first quarter in a long while. Not only was there the intifada; there was the American war on Iraq. When people have to seal their windows and send their kids to school with gas masks, for fear of a chemical attack, everything is put on hold. There was good cause for the fear, incidentally, because in the last war against Iraq, forty missiles fell on Israel.

Q: You must work with a lot of companies. Have any of them, or yourself, taken an active role in trying to influence the political leaders? I'm asking because there is a perception in America that the government is a puppet to big business.

Gaon: Hah, that's a laugh—on both fronts. First of all, the government is not afraid of big business. Politicians are looking for good headlines, and if the headline reads that they're crusading against the biggest business in the country, they don't care if they antagonize that business, because businesspeople have no teeth. Political consultants are far stronger in terms of influence. In your country, James Carville can change politics more than Bill Gates.

Conversely, most business leaders in this country are afraid to say openly what they think about the political situation, because they don't want to alienate a minister who has authority over an element of his business. So they will try to get a surrogate. Behind closed doors, business leaders will beg some champion of theirs to run for office; but the minute he announces his intention to run, the business leaders disappear.

Businessmen complain all the time about how the wrong politics hurt their business. But they're afraid to jump in and try to influence the politics; immediately they ask, how is this going to affect my business? Businesses want to be loved, not identified with a certain point of view; that's a great way to lose customers.

Q: Well, then, what kind of influence has the military had over business? I don't mean directly, but indirectly. When all of your employees are former military and active reservists, there's got to be an effect.

Gaon: The military can be both good and bad. If a bad personality enters it—the kind of guy who is a cutthroat competitor—the military will enhance that personality, and when he enters the business world, he'll be a very rough competitor, at the expense of everybody else. He'll also be a bad leader, because he won't attract the best of the business community, but the worst. The reverse is true: A good personality will also be enhanced.

Often those who were brave soldiers are terrible business leaders. In the army they depended on instant obedience, and they lead through intimidation. In the business world, you don't have people snapping at attention; you have to make them *want* to do something for you.

Q: And how do you do that?

Gaon: You lead by example. [Laughing] But, I guess, that's the military influence again.

Q: What would you point to as the biggest impact of the intifada?

Gaon: It's difficult to run a business when the decisions are always short term. But we cannot make long-term decisions in this uncertain environment. Also, there is a lack of hope. People do not see a light at the end of the tunnel.

Q: But, you're a CEO. Doesn't your board of directors, or whomever you report to, expect a confident, long-term plan from you every year?

Gaon: Any business leader here who stands before his investors and projects a 15 percent growth does so without believing it. There are many experienced CEOs here who tell their investors, "I don't believe growth will exceed 5 percent. The objective I'm challenging *my* workforce [to meet] is 10 percent. I don't think that will happen, but I will deliver that 5 percent."

Look, there is a lot less B.S. these days coming out of the corporate offices, because Israeli managers are realistic. Here, investors don't believe in the long-term plans; they believe in the manager. They say, "He or she has a record of making the right decisions, so we will go along."

In private companies, decisions are made on the intuition of the local managers. It's much easier to be a private company. During a time of terror, the business leaders in Israel make their decisions intuitively, from their own experience here, from their knowledge of the market and of the politics. I make decisions based on my experience and not on what's happening in the market.

And no business consultants will get the time of day from a CEO here, unless they have lived through this crisis. This is unlike anything else.

Q: Have you met investors who don't take the crisis into consideration and expect unreasonable returns?

Gaon: There are cases when global investors do not understand. They tell the local manager here, "I don't care how you do it, but make 15 percent profit." They don't care about the terror. And these local managers cut and fire, and cut some more, and eventually get fired themselves.

You have to remember this recession has been here for three years. We're already *done* with the cutting back; we're already *done* with streamlining operations; we've already sent people home. Things cannot get more efficient; they're efficient as hell now. What we have to do now is create. Smart managers are the ones who are investing, who are taking risks, who are looking at new opportunities. The companies that put finance people in charge are dead meat, because they're still obsessing over operational efficiency. The trend now is to put marketing people on top. The only way you can *create* something is to go into new areas.

The best investors are not saying, "Bring me 15 percent." The best investors are telling the local managers, "Let us help you with some marketing ideas."

I'll give you an example. Some businesses are now opening on Saturday, running the risk of a boycott from the Orthodox Israelis, which make up 20 percent of the population. We have one grocery store chain that not only is open on Saturday, but also sells pork—a double whammy. At least 50 percent of the Israelis are kosher only. Yet, they're making money.

Q: By the looks of things, the restaurants are making money, too.

Gaon: Some are. If you go out tonight, you won't believe there's a recession here. The restaurants and cafés are full. Israelis want to forget the terror and have a good time, so they go out. We think life is short and we feel like we should make the most of it.

That applies to business decisions, too. Right now I am advertising for a merged company that doesn't have government approval—and there's a real possibility they might not get it. Nonetheless, a decision had to be made, and this company and its investors couldn't wait. Like I say, life is short.

Q: You said earlier that many people here don't see a light at the end of the tunnel. Does that include you?

Gaon: It depends on how you define "peace." There will never be a complete victory over extremism, just as there will never be a total victory over organized crime. Have Americans defeated crime? No, but crime is controlled so that it is acceptable. The same can be done with terror.

In a way, I don't concern myself with those questions and the reasons why the economy is shrinking. What can I do about terror? So I focus on the economy, as bad as it is, because there I can do something.

■ ■ ■

MANAGING BY INSTINCT

After the interview with Moshe Gaon, I wondered if hiring an Israeli manager because of past performance in the crisis was any different from selecting a manager in an American company because of his track record. The difference, it seems, is in the weight given to experience in the Israeli business community. While an Israeli candidate interviewing for a new job would certainly lay out her vision for the fiscal year, it is likely that those listening would ascribe less importance to the question, "What are you going to do for us?" and more to, "What have you done for others during this crisis?" One's track record during a time of great unpredictability would be about the only indicator of performance in an unpredictable future.

Aggressive business plans, unless concretely anchored to past performance, would be just so much fodder in the interview process; the temptation would be to "cut to the chase" and examine one's past, rather than listen to someone's vision for the future. In fact, bold business plans would probably raise the red flag in the minds of senior management and actually undercut the candidate's case. Just as world-weary generals might evaluate a younger officer's fitness for a dangerous mission not on his thoughtful plan, but on his record of success in similar circumstances, Israeli executives know full well that the most thorough business plan might have to be altered the very next day in an economy under terrorist attack. Business leaders who have shown the flexibility and presence of mind to somehow prevail under chaotic conditions will have the edge. Although not a guarantor of victory, their selection represents the best guess of the older "veterans," who themselves have once successfully countered the unforeseen, and probably couldn't tell you how they did it.

The problem with "managing by instinct" is that it is more difficult to fully explain one's decisions, or to plan future responses, *or* to pass on to one's subordinates repeatable techniques for coping with crises. For those who picture the ideal CEO as a great communicator, visionary, and mentor, the Israeli model comes as something of a shock—as if a gunslinger had entered a contest between gentlemen target shooters. But managers reflect their times and their training. Israeli managers are in the midst of a terrorist economic siege and have been influenced, all, by some very dynamic leadership training, courtesy of the IDF. Battlefield training, which cultivates a frame of mind for coping with the unforeseen, is certainly appropriate to a business environment in which commuter buses, restaurants, and shopping malls are repeatedly bombed.

Just as importantly, military training puts the vaunted business plan in its proper place—as a "best guess," rather than a tool of enforcement to be wielded by senior management that's unhappy with the results of a subordinate. Anyone who has ever been coaxed by his manager into making a halfhearted prediction, and then had it later referred to as a *commitment* ("You *promised* me this result, and I passed it up the line"), knows how predictions can come back to haunt. It is highly unlikely an Israeli manager will be faulted for developing a plan that does not hold up to current events. He or she *will* be expected to outperform the competition, certainly; but just how that is accomplished may, at year's end, be something of a mystery.

CHAPTER FOUR

Checklist for Managing a Business Under Fire

- ❑ Develop the warrior mentality.
- ❑ Enforce, to the best of your ability, "business as usual."
- ❑ Cultivate flexibility of mind.
- ❑ Drill for terrorist attacks.
- ❑ Lead by personal example.
- ❑ Think like an owner.
- ❑ Never let the crisis become an excuse.
- ❑ Manage by instinct.

CHAPTER FIVE

The Unique Role of the Business Community

■ ■ ■

"I hate the idea that only generals and politicians are handling these issues. It's time for us businesspeople to take part."

—BENNY GAON, CEO, GAON HOLDINGS

THE BEST WEAPON THE ISRAELI BUSINESS COMMUNITY HAS IN the fight against terror is, unquestionably, continued high performance in the marketplace. Every business success denies the terrorists their victory and thereby adds sweetness to every new contract, sale, and customer. Although, as we have seen, Israeli businessmen do frequently fight terrorism in a literal sense, as activated reservists, the greatest contribution a manager can make is to maintain, and hopefully enhance, precrisis levels of production and service while the military prosecutes the actual defense of the economy. That said, there are other ways in which *only* the business community can combat terror. The measures taken have not been robust, like those of the Israel Defense Forces (IDF), and they have not made headlines, but they have been quietly effective, raising the hope that the terrorist problem will one day quit Israel—in the words of T. S. Eliot—"not with a bang, but a whimper."

■ ■ ■

Interview with Ram Caspi, Advocate, Caspi & Company

"This isn't a PR exercise.
We mean business."

During my two interviews at Egged Bus Company, I had expressed the hope of meeting with the legal firm representing Egged in its lawsuit against the terrorists. I was told with a smile of commiseration that Ram Caspi is the busiest attorney in the country, and that it was very unlikely an interview could be arranged in a few days or even weeks. I took my case to Yoram, hoping the good offices of the Ministry of Industry and Trade would help, but I was told it would be easier to arrange a meeting with Prime Minister Ariel Sharon himself than the most famous lawyer in Israel. Yoram promised to try, however, and I crossed my fingers. The very evening of the second Egged interview, I returned to the David Intercontinental and made use of the gym. There was another guest, besides myself, in the weight room, so I struck up a conversation. As it turned out, he wasn't a guest but a legal clerk whose office was nearby. I knew Ram Caspi's office was in Tel Aviv, so I asked, as casually as I could, for the name of the firm. He responded: "Caspi & Company." At that point, I nearly jumped for joy and began talking rapidly and earnestly. The young man, whose English couldn't keep up, politely backed away. I happened to catch myself in the workout-room mirror and realized what an unusual image I presented: a perspiring American in shorts and T-shirt talking a mile a minute and gesticulating wildly. I said, "Wait here," and ran to my room for my briefcase. Moshe, for that was his name, very fortunately remained in the gym and eventually listened to my story. He promised to talk to his boss on my behalf and, sure enough, I was granted an interview the next day with the legal lion of Israel.

As Yoram and I waited in the wood-paneled boardroom at Caspi & Company, I watched the front-office activity through the open door. Everything—the activity and the office layout—seemed to lead to a shut, massive, mahogany door, occasionally tapped by tiptoeing, deferential secretaries. Suddenly the door opened, letting out a cloud of bluish tobacco smoke. I saw a small man in his fifties in a blue double-breasted suit pacing about the thick office carpet, energetically puffing on a cigarette, and having a conversation in Hebrew with a speakerphone. The conversation ended and the door closed, then just as suddenly reopened, as if in afterthought, and Ram Caspi walked straight to us, offering cigarettes. I politely declined, and he shared a story with us.

Caspi: King Hussein and [Yitzhak] Rabin were both heavy smokers, you know. A few years ago, Rabin told me of a big meeting they both had with President Clinton and Hillary. As the meeting wore on, they looked in vain for the ashtrays. But there were no ashtrays. These two world leaders were afraid to ask, especially in front of Hillary, so they drummed their fingers on the table and fidgeted. After the meeting, King Hussein said to Rabin, "Quick, let's go to my room and smoke." And that's what they did.

Q: I'm so glad you've spared some time for me. Egged Bus Company's lawsuit against the terrorists, to the degree it is being reported in the United States, is described as a PR gesture, with little hope of collecting for damages.

Caspi: Not at all. This isn't a PR exercise. We mean business. And we're collecting.

Q: How did all this start?

Caspi: First of all, let me say that I'm a lefty when it comes to Israeli politics. I'm for peace. To some people, it might seem strange that a person with my political views is handling this case, but the surest way to further the cause of peace is to fight terror.

Except for Tel Aviv, where there is a competitor bus company, Egged handles about 90 percent of the Israeli passengers. They have been targeted by all the terrorist groups who are trying to intimidate the population.

We were instructed by Egged to see if a legal course of action could be pursued. But against whom? Can you sue someone who has blown himself up, along with innocent men, women, and children? No, he's dead. Can you sue his father and mother? No. Legally, you can fight only the Palestinian Authority. But that wasn't enough for us. We realized we had to hit the personal pockets of those who are responsible for sending terrorists into Israel. So I told the judge that we would also be suing Mr. Yasser Arafat personally.

The judge asked me why? I told him, you don't sue the corporation—you sue the CEO personally, because only then do you get his attention. He realizes, "They're going to attach my bank accounts, my house, my properties, etc." The judge agreed.

Q: Was it a hard case to make?

Caspi: You must be prepared. You may think you know everything, but when you come to a court of law, you have to produce evidence. And if you do not have the evidence, you will lose the case, even if the court believes you are right.

We had a number of things to prove. One, we had to prove the Palestinian Authority did not assume the responsibilities it agreed to assume by signing a number of international agreements, including the Oslo Accord. Two, we had to prove that either they were directly responsible for the terror, or that they did not prevent it when they easily could have—and, in fact, aided it through television broadcasting, the speeches of their leaders, etc.

Three, in order to show that Yasser Arafat was responsible personally, we had to show the court that he either instructed, financed, aided, or abetted terrorist activities. We were greatly helped by original documents, which have been captured—documents that show the movement of the money, with instructions as to how to carry out the terrorist attack, along with checks that were signed by Yasser Arafat. Do you remember that ship the Israeli navy captured in January 2002, with all of the weapons and bombs? That's where many of the checks, personally signed by Mr. Arafat, were found. There is a book by Dani Neveh, which goes into great detail of Arafat's sponsorship of terrorism. Unfortunately, I believe it's only available in Hebrew.

Q: Does somebody actually serve Arafat with papers? I'm trying to imagine that.

Caspi: The legal documents, under the Oslo agreement, are delivered to the Ministry of Justice in Jerusalem, and they deliver them to the lawyers of the Palestinian Authority.

Q: It must have been very gratifying to finally prove the connection.

Caspi: It's not enough to prove that the PA and Mr. Arafat were responsible. We had to establish damages. As far as Egged is concerned, it was rather easy to prove damages, because after each suicide bombing on a bus, the passenger flow dropped tremendously for a period of time, then slowly returned to the average rate. Then another bombing would happen, followed by another valley on the chart. We took the "valleys" and added up the damages. The Israeli government assisted Egged with 50 percent of the lost revenue, and we sued for the remaining 50 percent.

We sued for only one year—from October 2000 through October 2001. We are planning to sue for year two and for year three as well. There are many ways to fight terror. Military force is only one. You must close their accounts, attach personal assets, sue everybody involved.

Q: This is where I think many people, including myself, are surprised to hear that actual money was collected from the terrorists.

Caspi: How do we collect? According to the Oslo agreement, all importation into the Palestinian Authority passes through Israeli ports. Under the agreement, Israel must collect the customs duties and transfer it to the PA. So we are like a tax collector, on behalf of the Palestinians, but all the money goes to them.

We attached that money, up to the amount awarded by the court. The PA has challenged the verdict and will fail to dissuade the court because they don't have the evidence. The evidence has to speak for itself.

There has also been a verdict in Arafat's absence—he wouldn't appear in court—for about $12 million. Now, how do we collect from Arafat? Well, we have to find his personal assets, which will not be hard, and attach them in the amount awarded by the court.

Q: But what if it's in a Swiss bank account or someplace equally hard to access?

Caspi: There are international conventions—one is called the Law of Enforcement of Foreign Judgments. Let's say we found a bank account in Sweden. Sweden will honor the Israeli judgment, just as we would honor a judgment from a Swedish court of law. There is reciprocity among the civilized nations.

Q: Have there been other successful lawsuits against the terrorists?

Caspi: Yes, many of the insurance companies in Israel have joined in a lawsuit against the PA for about $140 million. Huge numbers of cars are being stolen in Israel and appearing in the West Bank. We discovered that thousands of Israeli cars have been *registered* in Gaza and Ramallah and [are] being used by members of the Palestinian Authority. The PA has admitted that as many as 5,000 Israeli cars have been registered, but the number is probably twice that.

But this is just the beginning. There will be a snowball. After the verdict in favor of Egged, one insurance company filed suit, then *all* the insurance companies filed suit. Hotels, restaurants, theaters will soon follow. This snowball could result in *billions* of dollars [of damages].

Q: The collection of damages has to be very satisfying, but are there other benefits to a lawsuit—for example, PR benefits on behalf of Israel?

Caspi: No, I don't think so. We have lost the war of world public opinion. The news reports are too influential.

Q: Before I forget, what did you do in the military?

Caspi: I was an officer in intelligence for three years, then served in the reserves until my fiftieth birthday.

Q: Is this case dangerous for you? I mean, if a U.S. attorney were suing the Mafia, he might be concerned about personal safety. And these terrorists are worse than the Mafia.

Caspi: I am not concerned. Everybody knows my political beliefs and knows I am doing my job.

Q: Aside from this unique case for Egged, has the business activity for even a famous lawyer suffered during this crisis?

Caspi: If anyone tells you they have not been affected by the intifada, they lie. Even this law office has suffered. There has been less investment, less deals made, less business during these last few years.

■ ■ ■

SUING THE TERRORISTS

Before this interview, the very idea of using society's most refined means of redress against murderous outlaws seemed ridiculous. One assumes a lawsuit to have two interested parties, plaintiff and defendant, both of whom show up in court and go through the lengthy process. The image of terrorists surrendering their arms to sit in the dock and answer questions that do not lend themselves to propagandistic replies is absurd. Even if one could stage a trial with appointed surrogates of the terrorists and gain a judgment, what would be the probability of collecting for damages from clandestine organizations that have evaded all attempts at capture?

Well, as I learned from Ram Caspi, the probabilities are rather high. How much damage a judgment really does to terrorists—considering the inexhaustible financial support they seem to enjoy, and the very low cost of assembling belt-bombs stuffed with nails and bolts—is open to question. But even without the prospect of collecting for damages, a lawsuit against the terrorist has great merit. As I left the offices of Caspi & Company, I couldn't help thinking that Ram may have underestimated the PR benefits of the Egged lawsuit and others like it. As an American, I certainly did not agree with Ram that Israel has "lost" in the court of public opinion. I thought he was being a bit hard on himself.

The beauty of a lawsuit against terrorists who harass Israeli society is that it returns the favor. There are few processes in life more harassing than legal action, especially if joined by numerous plaintiffs in a kind of national class-action suit. The Palestinian Authority represents itself as a legal institution; it cannot simply ignore the papers it's served with if it wishes to be taken seriously in other official matters, such as border disputes and peace negotiations. Attorneys must be hired and paid throughout the interminable processes. The prospect of endless litigation has prompted many a corporation, in its own mind innocent of the charges, to settle nevertheless, just to stop the bleeding. The most powerful corporations in the world tremble at the prospect of a major class-action suit. Why shouldn't the Palestinian Authority as it contemplates defending itself against numerous complaints from Israeli insurance companies, hotel associations, and restaurants? Egged's pending cases for the years 2002, 2003, and 2004 must give the PA cause for worry after the litigation proved successful on the first pass. The PA is in a somewhat unique position in that it is vulnerable to collection via customs fees. Monetary awards aside, the ordeal of litigation without end can be exhausting. Attorney jokes aside, the terrorists may have met their match in the Israeli trial lawyer.

Lawsuits also become self-perpetuating news stories. Every step in the legal process merits another entry in the press, another mention on the air, another retelling of the grievance before the public. From a media standpoint, lawsuits have legs. What chance was there, for example, of the public ever forgetting the bombing of Pan Am 103 over Lockerbie, Scotland when periodic news updates of the suit against Moammar Gadhafi were broadcast? Well-publicized legal actions tend to unite the civilized world around the plaintiff, because only the civilized world recognizes the option of litigation. The terrorist is suddenly put on the defensive; his bluff has been called. He has been crying for justice, now here is the forum. He must answer questions that cannot be dealt with through diatribe. The plaintiff has documented his case, and only evidence to the contrary will refute it. A court of law is not a room full of sycophant reporters eager for a provocative sound bite. There is only an implacable, incorruptible judge, and all evidence must be laid before the bar of reason. Should there be a judgment against the terrorist (yet another news story) his hand is forced; the world will see that he does not recognize the justice and the "equality before the law" he has purportedly been fighting for. It is no wonder that terrorists, who welcome every public relations opportunity and who bask in the limelight of the news media, refuse to appear in their own defense.

It would diminish the significance of the Egged suit to consider it a success simply because of the collected damages. Even if a penny had not been recovered, such legal actions are victories for the civilized world, making it much more difficult for the terrorists to garner the moral support they seek from other nations. No fair-minded person could listen to the spokespeople of the PA again, without recalling the outcome of the case. Egged, by fighting terrorism *in the courtroom*, furthered the cause for peace and hastened the day to an economic revival. If Ram Caspi is correct about the "snowball effect," the Palestinian Authority will be forced to choose between two very different futures—one fraught with unending litigation, the other free of the tyranny of the terrorists.

Well-publicized court action against terrorists helps the Israeli case in the battle for public opinion in other ways. Few people can complain of excessive force because the use of force is abdicated; the outcome is in the hands of a judge or jury. If the terrorist is found to be innocent, the plaintiff has lost and has no recourse. The Israeli team is taking a great chance, and the world takes note. A lawsuit may also expose the supporters of terrorism who prefer anonymity, which also helps swing public opinion. A judgment can prepare the way for government action, such as freezing the assets of individuals or a group; it can even be a reference point for military action down the road that will be accepted by many as proper justification. And a successful suit like Egged's is a gesture of moral support for the surviving victims and relatives of victims of the bombings. Had Egged not pursued those guilty of sponsoring the multiple murders of its passengers, customer loyalty—perhaps even investor loyalty—might have diminished.

The Egged case is not without precedent. The Dan and Isrotel hotel chains, along with dozens of individual Israeli hotels, sued the

Iraqi government after the first Gulf War. The forty or so Scud missiles that fell on Israel caused negligible damage. The high tensions, however, emptied the hotels. In an encapsulated, thankfully brief period of time, Israeli hotel owners were to get a foretaste of what was to come a decade later. The Gulf War tourist crisis lasted a couple of months, not years, but even that was sufficient time to cost the industry hundreds of millions of dollars in lost revenue. Here again, you might have thought the odds of collecting one penny from Saddam Hussein, who launched the missiles, were so slim as not to justify the meticulous paperwork required by the United Nations commission to document damages. Many hotels, in fact, did not participate in the suit. I remember Ami Hirschstein, CEO of the thirteen-hotel Dan chain, placing the odds at 80–20 against winning. Nonetheless, a 20 percent chance of recovering tens of millions of dollars in lost revenue seemed a chance worth taking.

Just as the Palestinian Authority had been exposed to collection by virtue of its dependence on the Israeli customs authorities, Hussein was similarly vulnerable because several foreign bank accounts were seized. The U.N. commission eventually awarded the Israeli hotels millions of dollars in damages. It took a while, five to six years, but the money was collected, and Hirschstein's 20 percent hunch paid off. Other businesses, Egged Bus Company for one, took note: Even one of the world's most notorious villains, protected by armies, can be forced to undergo the humiliation of having to pay millions of dollars to those he has wantonly attacked.

Interview with Oded Tyrah, President, Phoenicia America-Israel (Flat Glass) Ltd.

"Businesspeople by themselves could have made peace. Business is a language even enemies can speak—as long as everybody gains from the transaction."

I met Oded Tyrah late in the evening, after he had presided over a meeting of the Manufacturers Association of Israel. He is president of that association and of Phoenicia Glass, the country's largest exporter of "flat" glass—the kind used in high-rise office buildings and shopping malls. He is in his early sixties, about five-feet-seven, wiry, and—like every other Israeli executive I had met—very fit. Oded was a general in the IDF, and he has fought in a number of wars as a paratrooper, then as an artillery commander. He is one of the nation's most recognized business leaders.

Q: General, how has a company like Phoenicia, which is dependent on the health of the construction industry, fared during this crisis?

Tyrah: You don't have to call me "general."

Q: I don't get to talk to a general very often. I just wanted to make the most of it.

Tyrah: [Laughing] Okay. Our biggest response to the years of terror here was to become an exporter. After the first intifada, which hit the local economy pretty hard, demand for glass went down. People were building [fewer] office buildings and restaurants. There was less investment. So we decided to change our business strategy. We decided to become an exporter [and] less dependent on local economic conditions. Instead of selling 90 percent to the local market, we built a huge plant in Galilee, and now we sell 82 percent of our product abroad, where our customers are less affected by terror. We were able to move the center of gravity from one market to another.

Our original vision was to sell to Israel, Jordon, Syria, Lebanon, Saudi Arabia, and Egypt. But that never happened. Now we sell to Greece, Turkey, Italy, Mexico, Australia, Belgium, Russia, Spain, and South Africa.

Q: Does that mean you bequeath the local market to your competitors?

Tyrah: No, if the local market picks up, we sell here first. If it slows down, we sell abroad. But, the point is, now we have that option.

Q: Have you ever had issues with your global customers questioning your ability to deliver on time, due to the intifada?

Tyrah: Delivery is everything. We have competitors in the Far East. Their prices are lower, but they're never on time. So being on time was our major suit. Then came the intifada and, yes, customers were wondering if we could still deliver. In the construction industry, even one or two days off schedule can cost the builder huge amounts of money. We *had* to keep our timetable and our reputation for being there when they needed us.

Q: A lot of the hotel managers I have interviewed have done some major restructuring to cope with low occupancies. Does your company look different today because of the crisis, or are you pretty much the same—the major difference being a global client base?

Tyrah: Here we were—far from the markets, with more transportation and packaging costs, and under frequent attack. We knew we had to reduce operating costs, which means we had to initially spend money on new technologies like laser systems, robotics, and vision systems. It's like science fiction in our factories today. We have a laser system scanning the ribbon of glass coming out of the factory. If there is an imperfection, a robot will mark the point on the glass. The vision system—high-tech cameras—sees the mark and tells the robot not to accept that portion of glass.

We employed 500 workers five years ago; now we're down to 300. And these 300 [employees] had to be upgraded through another investment in training. This gave us the immunity to withstand the current intifada.

Q: What about those who didn't develop "immunity"? Have some of your competitors gone by the wayside?

Tyrah: Everyone has suffered. We have an unemployment pool of 280,000 people in Israel. That's a huge number for such a small country. If you count the families of these people, that represents close to a *million* people who are affected by these times of trouble.

You'll always have some unemployment due to technical upgrades. When I installed robotics, I suppose I contributed some to the unemployment. But then, on top of that, we have the intifada. To fight both of these influences, you need a growth rate of 6 percent or 7 percent, and we're at 2 percent. That requires investment, and investment is going down.

The global investors will put their money at the place of the best return. We have to attract the money—not necessarily the people—and that's a very tough task, especially now.

Q: Do your people expect you, as a former general, to be right all the time when it comes to strategic decision making?

Tyrah: [Laughing] I hope not. But the military experience helps. Today we live in a global village. Someone pees in Indonesia and the sea level rises in Israel. Things happening all over the world affect our business. At any time, somebody can come up with a technological leap and we will be suddenly left behind. The less natural advantages you have, the more vigilant you have to be.

It's the same on the battlefield: Things change very fast. Information must be fed to your staff so they can adjust the battle plan. That's how businesses are run today. In business schools, I can see that they are now teaching things we learned in the army many years ago.

Today, in Israel, it's a continuous decision-making process. In the past, you made a strategic decision and it was good for seven years. That was the direction of the company, implemented by a seven-year plan. Today, you make a "strategic decision" and you may change it within three months. Every moment you get information that will affect your original decision.

So we have to be very flexible. You cannot sell in your home market, so you go abroad. Things change there; you must respond. A customer leaves you because he doesn't like Israelis, [so] you must find another customer.

Q: Are customers that blatant?

Tyrah: In Belgium, Norway, and France, Israeli products are sometimes taken off the shelf. Sometimes we don't label the product Made in Israel.

And, of course, in the Middle East the same thing happens. We have made the case that a boycott will in the end hurt many Arabs, who are employed in Israeli factories along the border and inside some Arab countries. If they are unemployed, the peace process will be endangered.

If you punish the business sector, you punish the strongest supporter of the peace process.

Q: How much influence can the business community exert on the political situation?

Tyrah: We can talk to each other, when the politicians are not talking to other politicians. One day I went to Ramallah—a very dangerous place—with some Palestinian customers of mine. We went in their car to a restaurant; they brought us roast pigeons to eat. My customer said to me: "Peace may be a long time coming. Let's sell and buy glass between the events."

I go to business forums, the same forums the Palestinian businesspeople attend. We talk, we go to lunch, we know each other. As long as the politicians aren't there, we get along. Businesspeople are friends.

I'll tell you a funny story. I was at an international business conference when tensions were high. Some Palestinian members asked for a vote to throw the Israeli contingent out of the organization. All hell broke loose; there was much debating and voices were loud. But the vote was against their proposal. Then we had lunch. At the table were the *same* Palestinians who had tried to throw us out. We were laughing and telling stories. I heard the Algerian minister say, "I don't understand these people."

Businesspeople by themselves could have made peace. Business is a language even enemies can speak—as long as everybody gains from the transaction. If only one party gains, the other feels exploited, and you're no better off.

Q: If, God forbid, we start experiencing terror attacks in the United States, how should our business leaders react?

Tyrah: Well, they should support the politicians who push for intelligence budgets. Eighty percent of our resources are put in intelligence, not in soldiers on the ground. That's how we nip in the bud the vast majority of terrorist attacks.

I was very impressed by the way Americans responded to 9/11. I think that you can appeal to that sense of patriotism by telling people to go out and to live, and to buy, and to enjoy life and not let the terrorists win.

And export! America's exports are only 10 percent of the GDP; ours are at 45 percent. That's why I'm so against strikes. They're like mini-strokes or heart attacks, which stop the blood flowing. When nearly half of your GDP is exported, you can't afford to stop the flow of blood even for a day.

Q: Do you see a light at the end of the tunnel for the Israeli economy?

Tyrah: Yes, but our well-being cannot be based on peace. Our companies have to be successful under any conditions; otherwise, other people have the ability to influence our way of life. We have to live our lives the way we want, whether there is peace or not.

■ ■ ■

BUSINESS AS A UNIVERSAL LANGUAGE

The image of Oded Tyrah and his Palestinian counterpart meeting over lunch—in the West Bank of all places, and in the midst of the intifada—is heartening and inspiring. It goes without saying that both men took personal risks: one simply for being an Israeli in the wrong place at the wrong time, the other for risking the possibility of being considered a collaborator—a "crime" that has frequently been punished by lynching in the West Bank. It seems as if, despite the dangers, they had a good time; whenever someone remembers the dish (roast pigeons), it usually means it was enjoyed. If two warring factions had sent out official emissaries in order to discover points of mutual interest, they could not have done better. The topic at hand was *business,* and nothing could be less controversial. Businesspeople do not disagree on the principle of free trade; only the terms may be temporarily in question, hence the expression "let's get down to business." Hatreds and prejudices have no place at the table because businesspeople are always looking forward for ways to reap mutual benefits. And every business transaction is an exchange of trust, enforced by long memories. While a politician may make treaties with questionable characters, no business professional will make a deal with someone who has cheated him before. Conviviality, mutual benefits, and trust—these three *prerequisites* of every successful business transaction are often conspicuously absent in political negotiations.

That this transaction had to be completed under the duress of the intifada is evidence, I think, that business does not pull the strings of political leaders. If it were so, there would have been no intifada, because the business communities on both sides of the issues have too much to lose by perpetuating the conflict. Instead, like hapless bartenders unable to quell a brawl in a Wild West saloon, they must stand clear for their own safety, and sadly watch the damages mount.

The economic conference is another example of the possibility of private geniality between public adversaries. One minute the Palestinians and Israelis are at loggerheads; the next, they are laughing and apparently enjoying each other's company over lunch. This is not unusual. American politicians posture in fierce debates for the benefit of their constituencies, and then break bread with the very opponent you could have sworn was an enemy. It seems that at this conference, too, once the public session was over, there was a genuine acceptance of one another that could have been further cultivated. How? Through actual business relationships, as opposed to forums where business is *talked about* but not consummated. The parties were only a tantalizing step away from true interdependence—the symbiotic relationship of business partners. It could probably be argued that, to the degree to which deals were struck, the need for formal "conferences" would no doubt diminish; everyone would be too busy making money.

There is a dark side, however, to the normally commendable yearning for peace and prosperity on the part of businesspeople the world over. There have been occasions where the business community has willfully ignored the barbaric penchants of the political leaders of their trading partners. About the only Americans who opposed war with Hitler in 1941, for example, were businesspeople who thought the differences between the nations were resolvable through continued commerce. Similarly, Saddam Hussein had European business partners who were willing to overlook his intentions while supplying him with technology that could easily be converted to further his military ambitions.

Although business is a universal language, it doesn't speak "terrorism." There is no win-win in supplying terrorists with the means to kill one. Fortunately, in the case of Israeli-Palestinian relations, there are those in the West Bank who would give anything to return to the days when Palestinians crossed freely into Israel, made a decent wage, and returned to their homes—in other words, when they were able to earn and claim a stake in the economy. The businesspeople on both sides of this conflict are trying to reestablish normal relations, and they are among the most agreeable when it comes to the concessions required of both sides for a permanent peace.

▪ ▪ ▪

Interview with Benny Gaon, CEO, Gaon Holdings

"Just imagine four or five industrial zones, located on the Israeli and Palestinian borders, where both can work together."

Often I would show my interview itinerary to the executives and managers I met with, to get their reactions and to show them they were in good company. Invariably, as eyes scanned down the list, I would hear a comment like, "Ah, Benny Gaon," followed by an affirmative nodding of the head. More than one interviewee informed me that "gaon" translates from Hebrew into *genius.* "You mean," I would ask, "his name is Benny Genius?"

Invariably the answer was, "Yes, you will be interviewing a genius."

With a ready laugh, Gaon began our interview by translating his last name for me. He is one of the country's most prominent business leaders, to be sure—the chairman and founder of a renowned capital investment firm and billion-dollar company. He is chairman of the board or director of no less than seventeen other Israeli companies, and he is, incidentally, the father of Moshe Gaon, the ad agency executive interviewed in Chapter 4. Benny Gaon is an extremely engaging personality. I could see at once why he has been chosen by political leaders of both the right and the left as an emissary to the regimes of the Middle East. In his office there are autographed photographs on the wall of a number of world leaders, past and present.

Q: Can we start with the major impact of the current intifada, as you see it?

Gaon: Sure. In Israel, we have just two natural resources: sand and brains. We developed a great high-tech market, and our companies were modeled after the American and European companies. Four years ago, there was a big wave of foreign investment. The Western investors had better communication with companies here in Israel, because we were like companies they have always dealt with. So, things were good; we all felt as if we were moving ahead. Then came the intifada and, suddenly, everything stopped. Investors said to themselves, "I'll put my money in Ireland."

Not only was it difficult to get foreign investment dollars, but many *Israeli* investors started looking elsewhere. Two years ago, Israelis transferred $1.5 billion to Swiss banks. They said it was safer.

The important thing is not what changes have taken place since the intifada—it's *what changes have to come.* In my opinion, there will be no major movement in the Israeli economy until there is a settlement of the political issues. This is a country without a corporate strategy, and unless more business leaders get involved in advising the government, or running for office, nothing will change.

So this is where we are. We see no change. And the mood of business has suffered. The enthusiasm is gone. After a terrorist attack, no one is in the frame of mind to get excited even about a very exciting business deal. The attitude is, "Let's wait a few weeks and see what happens."

Q: Is it hard, then, to see through or beyond this crisis?

Gaon: After an attack, yes, you don't look into the future; you look around you and make sure your family members are all okay. Everybody is on their cell phones. Then you read the paper or watch the news. Since it's a small country, you know one of the victims, or at least you know his or her family.

These attacks happen over and over again. More than a thousand Israelis have been murdered during this current intifada. That doesn't put you in a creative state of mind for business.

And the demoralizing thing is, you don't know how to fight it. How do you stop a suicide bomber? It's not just a military solution. Look at the Americans in Iraq: coalition soldiers everywhere, armed to the teeth, yet every second day there is a suicide bombing and they can't stop it. We have one of the most advanced militaries in the world, but can you stop a suicide bomber with an F-16?

Q: Can the business community stop a suicide bomber?

Gaon: Perhaps. If he has a stake in the economy, if he has something to lose—a job, a savings account, a house, and a family that is being supported—perhaps he won't come over here with a bomb strapped to his belt. On the other hand, if he has nothing to lose, he might.

I tell you, I hate the idea that only generals and politicians are handling these issues. It's time for us businesspeople to take part. We must privatize the peace process.

Q: Can you give a practical example of what the business community can do?

Gaon: I will. And your country did it! Look at the "duty-free zone" concept in Jordan. Before the American involvement in the free-zone concept, Jordanian exports to America were $40 million worth of products a year. After three years, it jumped to $400 million. That means the people in Jordan are working, saving, and looking forward to the future—all because American business interests got involved.

Just imagine four or five industrial zones, located on the Israeli and Palestinian borders, where both can work together. I am developing a project now, and I'm getting together Swedish, Israeli, Palestinian, and American investors. We provide the jobs, mainly for the Palestinians, and you provide the market. We make furniture, for example, and IKEA says: "We will buy the furniture you make." We've got the jobs, but not the market. Bring me IKEA, or another company that will commit to buying the products we make, and we will fill 50,000 jobs just in one zone. It is a win-win solution. No donations, no charity, just good business for all. And now you would have 50,000 Palestinian men gainfully employed, instead of standing around the street corners without money.

Provide us the markets; we'll provide the merchandise.

Q: Is there a precedent for a successful industrial zone?

Gaon: Of course. In Erez, near Gaza, 10,000 Palestinians are making clothing, chairs, and toys, in multiple small factories, even through this intifada. And it's working! Private investors put up the money. A wealthy Palestinian living in Europe is afraid to invest in Palestine for a lot of reasons: lack of security, fears of corruption. But he feels comfortable investing in a project on the border, in which Israelis and other countries are involved. Shirts, pants, furniture, consumer goods—nothing high tech. But bring us the market to absorb what we make.

Q: Are these Palestinians being pressured by the terrorists not to work in the industrial zone?

Gaon: No. Because Arafat is getting a commission on the business. [Grinning] I told you this was win-win.

Q: Why would these investors be so eager to participate in an industrial zone when, as you say, many of them are putting their money elsewhere, in less troubled economies?

Gaon: Actually, the Swedish investors came to me. The Swedish Industry Association came here and asked, "How can we help in the peace process?" So I told them we don't need charitable donations—half of it ends up in the hands of the wrong people, anyhow. I told them, "All we need from you is the market." I talked about the success of Erez and how that concept can work in other places along the border. In a few weeks, some Palestinian businesspeople and I are going to meet with the Swedish [investors] in Stockholm.

Q: I'm curious. Have you ever been in danger because of your visits to the Palestinian side?

Gaon: It's all relative. Years ago, Rabin sent me to Tunisia. I traveled incognito, and I was nervous as hell. That was the first time I met with Arafat. He's not the most personable guy in the world, but you can at least *talk* to him. I told him I was more "Palestinian" than he was, because I was born in Jerusalem. But, yes, that was a scary trip. Later, I traveled to Jordan to meet King Hussein. Now, you have to understand, he was a legend to me, and I was genuinely awed when I came to his palace. He asked me, "Have you had lunch? Come, let's eat." He led me to a banquet room. It was beautiful, very luxurious. I asked him, "Your Majesty, this is my first time with a king. Tell me how to behave." He answered, "Take your fork and knife, and eat."

■ ■ ■

SETTING THE MOOD FOR BUSINESS

The concept of industrial zones will be taken up after the next interview, which will also shed light on the successful Erez model. On some reflection, though, I think Benny's comments on the intifada's effects on the emotional state of the business community were rather touching. He was the first person I interviewed to state the problem in such simple and poignant terms. One *does* have to be "in the mood" for business. And if a natural optimist such as Benny Gaon cannot, in the aftermath of a terrorist's attack, be cheered by an otherwise exciting investment opportunity, then the problem must be endemic in the Israeli business community. Very often, the rank and file of a given company does not share the unbridled enthusiasm of the owner or CEO, anyway. If the owner of a business cannot get excited, how can you expect more of his associates? There have been so many terrorist attacks in Israel over the last few years, one wonders if the business community has been "in the mood" since October 2000.

I wondered briefly if the American phenomenon of "blue Monday" would be in any way analogous. American managers have to cope with a certain lack of enthusiasm on the part of employees who have had a long, and perhaps overindulgent, weekend. The irony is that while the American employee would rather be elsewhere on Monday, Israeli employees may find sanctuary at the workplace and be fairly content to go about their duties. They are "blue" for other reasons. How does a manager raise the spirits of a workforce whose joy of life has been dampened by years of mass murder in the streets, malls, and restaurants?

If one wanted to set the mood for romance, candles, music, and a glass of wine might be a good place to start. Managers who wish to create a workplace atmosphere that generates excitement would be well advised to begin with the trappings of a dynamic business day. No matter how poorly a company may be doing in the midst of recession, there is *always* good news to be found somewhere in the operations. That news should be charted or graphed and posted on the wall, lest employees be given the erroneous impression that everything is going badly. Brainstorming sessions, in which the input of even the most reluctant is solicited, is a great way to start the creative juices flowing. Recognition awards and the sharing of the accompanying success stories can inspire the performance of observers and recipients alike. Opportunities on the horizon should be the topic of group discussions. Teams should be developed, if only on the flimsiest of pretexts, so that the solitary can contribute to, and be buoyed by, a task force greater than the sum of its parts. Managers—by no means immune to the dispiriting effects of current events—must try to rise above their personal problems and lead by example.

It is not an exaggeration to suggest that some of the high points in many people's lives are work related. Not many professionals would agree with the adage, "The worst day fishing beats the best day working." One's work can and in fact must be exciting, if the company is to survive an economic crisis. The worse the situation on the outside, the more the manager must strive "on the inside" to generate enthusiasm for the task at hand. A paycheck is not sufficient cause for performance above and beyond the call of duty. Employees must be excited, and creation of that state of mind is definitely a managerial challenge, even under normal conditions. Under abnormal conditions, such as a terrorist crisis, the manager's role as cheerleader becomes even more crucial.

■ ■ ■

Interview with Gaby Bar, Deputy Director, Ministry of Industry and Trade

"In the Middle East,
I'm afraid politics still leads business."

On our way back to the Ministry of Industry and Trade in Jerusalem, Yoram took me to the Western Wall of the Temple Mount. I had expected hundreds of people, but this being a weekday, there wasn't much of a crowd at all. For an American, writing a business book with the terrorist crisis as the context, I couldn't help looking at this site as the trigger point for the current intifada. On September 27, 2000, Ariel Sharon entered the Temple Mount as a gesture of defiance, reacting to newspaper reports that then Prime Minister Ehud Barak was willing to consider, in principle, giving up control of the sacred mountain. Although every Israeli I interviewed believed that the intifada would have begun without this provocation, this was the moment the "terrorist crisis"—as reported by the news media since October 2000—began. My eyes involuntarily scanned the tops of the walls and structures around me. Soldiers with automatic weapons were everywhere, although they seemed more interested in the female visitors to the wall than developing threats. Their complacency, in fact, was quite comforting. Feeling safe, I listened to Yoram's history of the site and, as an American, mentally hoped for a peaceful solution for all concerned in this age-old conflict. Sometimes, I reflected, it's good to live in the New World, where there are few, if any, legacies of conflict to burden successive generations.

I was looking forward to this interview with Gaby Bar, whom Yoram had informed me was an expert on qualifying industrial zones (QIZs), which are, in effect, duty-free manufacturing areas. Industrial zones in general, and a QIZ in particular, are examples of the government turning to the Israeli business community for help in the peace process—and of the business community fighting terror in its own unique way.

Q: Was the concept of an industrial zone created in reaction to the intifada?

Bar: Yes and no. We didn't need industrial zones before the intifada because 150,000 Palestinians worked in Israel, in all kinds of businesses—mostly in agriculture, construction, and services, but some in industry as well. That number now is, for practical purposes, zero, because no one is allowed to cross the border. Israel used to sell $2.7 billion a year into Palestine, and they would sell nearly a million [dollars' worth of products] to us. Now, both figures are cut in half.

A factory complex on the Palestinian side was launched in 1999, financed by the World Bank and donor countries, including Israel. It was called the Gaza industrial zone and amounted to a hundred factories located in the town of Karni. As soon as the intifada was let loose, this industrial zone became a battlefield. There were shootings and stabbings. Six or seven Israelis had factories there and lost their investments. The Israeli government had encouraged these businesspeople to invest in Karni then, after the intifada, prevented them, for their own safety, from going to see their investments. Needless to say, many in the business community looked askance at the whole idea of investing in an industrial zone.

The lesson learned was that you need to have an Israeli security solution, which meant the zone should also be on the Israeli border. Remember, Karni is in the West Bank.

Q: So, then, Erez is protected by Israeli soldiers?

Bar: Yes, that complex is on the border, in the white zone, which is a kind of "no-man's-land." There is an entrance on both the Israeli and

Palestinian side. To work there, a Palestinian must be at least twenty-eight years old with a family. There are inspection checkpoints on the way in.

There are three main reasons for the success in Erez: One, it's on the border. Two, it's secured by Israel Defense Forces, and three, inexpensive labor. More and more companies are coming to Erez. Here we are, in the midst of the intifada, and Israeli and Palestinian businessmen are planning the expansion of Erez. We have already 173 companies; half of them are owned by Palestinians. Half are textiles [sewing] and one-third are carpentry shops making furniture.

Thousands of Palestinians work there, along with Israelis. It's a cosmos unto itself. People get along.

Q: How can the terrorists abide such a successful Israeli-Palestinian operation?

Bar: The terrorists threatened the laborers not to go to work, but the internal pressures built. People needed jobs, and that need was stronger than their fear of the terrorists. So, some brave Palestinian laborers reported for work, and the terrorists looked the other way. Then more reported. Now it's a dynamic operation and the terrorists leave it alone; they don't officially recognize it, but they leave it alone. Those Palestinians who work there are not considered by the terrorists as collaborators.

That pressure works both ways, incidentally. During the tense times, the Israeli forces prohibited Palestinians from bringing anything with them into the facility, including their lunches, for the very legitimate fear of bombs. Well, that didn't last too long. The laborers complained enough and pressured their managers, and now they bring their lunch—which is checked, by the way.

Q: And half of the companies are owned by Palestinians?

Bar: Yes, and even some of the factories that are not owned outright by Palestinians have Palestinian partners. There is even a Palestinian-owned car repair garage that works on—and maintains—Israeli army cars! There is another Palestinian company that makes kosher ice cream. There are Palestinian supervisors and managers. Promotion is open to all. And people get along! We get best wishes phone calls from the Palestinians we work with on our holy holidays, and we call them on Ramadan.

Q: What is the difference between a QIZ and an industrial zone?

Bar: The qualifying industrial zone was created in 1995, when we made peace with Jordan. We had a free-trade agreement with the United States. Factories like Delta and Magal opened factories in Jordan, but when they tried to sell their products to the U.S., there was a problem. Whenever you have a free-trade agreement, you have to identify the place of origin of the products. Otherwise, products could be smuggled into Israel from another country and be sold under a false presumption. The reverse is true: Products could be smuggled into America from across the border and be sold to Israel, so rules of origin had to be defined. These rules are mostly based on added value. Sewing, for example, is added value to fabrics; it falls under the category of "substantial transformation." So clothes sewn in Jordan were subject to duties and quotas. Something had to be done, because Jordan did not have a free-trade agreement with the United States. So, those manufacturing areas in Jordan became "qualifying" industrial zones.

The effect was very dramatic. In 1997, Jordan exported $15 million worth of goods to the U.S. In 2002—*during the intifada*—their exports to the United States rose to $500 million, and the following year to $650 million. Twenty-five thousand new jobs were created, thanks to this QIZ.

Q: But, if the factories are not on the border, who guarantees the security?

Bar: Jordan does. By guaranteeing the security, they're helping to guarantee the peace.

Q: What a great example of business leading politics!

Bar: Yes, but unfortunately, there are more examples of politics leading business. An Egyptian businessman returning from Israel is given the third degree by the Egyptian authorities. An Israeli businessman who wants to go to Egypt is often rejected, for no reason.

There is the famous case of an Israeli technician named Azam. He is a Druz, which is a non-Jewish Israeli. He used to go into Egypt to fix refrigeration units. Then, one day, arbitrarily, he was put into jail for seventeen years as a spy! Now . . . do you want to go into Egypt to work on a machine? In the Middle East, I'm afraid politics still leads business.

▪ ▪ ▪

POSTSCRIPT ON EREZ: SUICIDE BOMBING, JANUARY 14, 2004

The industrial complex in Erez is not immune from terror attacks, even though over 10,000 Palestinians work inside. Two months after my return from Israel, I read in the papers of a suicide bombing at this very site. A young woman approached the security checkpoint, hobbling and in apparent pain. She told the Israeli security team (four young men) that because of a metal pin in her knee, she could not cross the metal detector. According to established procedures, she was taken aside while a female security officer was sent for to do a physical check. At that point, she detonated, killing herself and the four Israelis. Both Hamas and the Al-Aqsa Martyrs Brigades immediately took credit. The article also referenced an earlier terrorist attack, in June 2003, in which four Israeli soldiers were killed and five more were wounded. Sporadic mortar attacks were also cited during that year. I should point out that none of the articles I read even hinted at the significance of the Erez industrial complex; one simply got the impression it was a troubled border crossing. The great work that goes on inside was not considered worth mentioning by the media.

One can see why Erez would be such a thorn in the side of the terrorists. The industrial complex hearkens back to the days when hundreds of thousands of Palestinians crossed freely into Israel to work. That number has been reduced, for obvious reasons of security, to the 10,000 or so who work inside the guarded complex. But even that reduced workforce threatens the ambitions of the terrorists, who cannot abide the spectacle of Palestinians working in harmony with Israelis. Nor do they condone the profitable partnerships between the Israelis and Palestinian business leaders, who have made the factories available. But Erez perseveres and, if Benny Gaon's and Gaby Bar's vision materializes, there will be more industrial complexes created on the borders, providing jobs for thousands more Palestinians who are caught in the middle of this crisis.

GETTING BUSINESSES INVOLVED

It remains to be seen if the concept of industrial zones will be the last gasp of well-meaning investors or the key to regional economic prosperity. It certainly seems to have been one of the best kept secrets of the Middle East. I had no idea tens of thousands of Palestinians worked in harmony, alongside Israelis, day after day, nor could I have guessed that Jordanian exports to the United States have skyrocketed. If one goes by the news media, the movers and shakers in the Middle East are the terrorists. Admittedly, they are the "shakers," but hopefully not for long. The "movers" are the Israeli and Palestinian businesspeople who quietly patch up the damage to the economy while the terrorists steal all the headlines.

An industrial zone is what happens when the peace process is turned over to the business community. The solution is typical of the free spirit in free enterprise. There are no treaties to ratify and no political parties to placate for support. When business gets into the act, the arrangement is quite simple: Here are the factories; let's get to work. The result is 10,000 Palestinians working alongside Israelis in a protected sanctuary of self-interest. Everybody wins—the Israeli and Palestinian investors, and the laborers and managers. The only losers are the terrorists, who now have a difficult time spreading messages of hate to Palestinians who eat their lunch every day with Israeli coworkers.

Even a single industrial zone is anathema to the terrorists because it is a publicly viewed time capsule of the way things were before the intifada, when Palestinians entered and left Israel freely. The prospect of a half dozen more industrial zones must be horrifying; they would mean a virtual return to the "old days" of mutual prosperity. Another frustration would be the inability of the terrorists to penetrate these highly secure areas or to intimidate Palestinians into not participating. By what means could hundreds of thousands of laborers be persuaded to give up their jobs? Acts of terror against Palestinians—the very population the terrorists claim to represent—would only destroy whatever moral support exits in the community. On the other hand, allowing the industrial zones to prosper *also* threatens public support for extremism. Terrorists do not want the "angry young men" required for their movement to be gainfully employed or to have a stake in the future. Either way, the terrorists are caught between a rock (the Israeli business community) and a hard place (the Palestinian business community). The industrial zone is very similar to a business alliance that locks out, and eventually starves out, a competitor—in this case, a "competitor" for the hearts and minds of the workforce.

The whole point of the industrial zone is, however, not philanthropic. Investors must find the return on the dollar worthwhile or they'll put their money elsewhere. In the case of Erez, the only model on the Israeli border, it seems as if investment is both protected and propitiously placed, considering the significant expansion about to unfold. The prospective investor should bear in mind that there is another sociological movement in the West Bank that's unreported by the press but of great importance to the investor. Nearly four years of widespread unemployment has created tremendous pressure on the Palestinian people, having had the effect of a prolonged labor strike, which now enjoys only halfhearted support. An emotionally conflicted but willing workforce awaits the opening of new industrial zones as Palestinians are eager to return to productive lives. And there is absolutely nothing the terrorists can do about it. Investors today could be on the ground floor of a regional economic revival, even if the intifada continues, unabated. In the words of Gaby Bar, the industrial zone is a "cosmos unto itself," protected by the IDF and ringing inside with the sounds of productivity. If only more investments were to be so sheltered against negative influences!

■ ■ ■

Interview with Adam Friedman, Venture Capitalist, Friedman-Associates

"There are more Israeli companies listed on the NASDAQ than from any other country."

One look at Adam Friedman's office and I recognized a man after my own heart. This was a working man's office, with papers and folders piled on the desk. He is the principal of a venture capital firm with many investments in Israel. Adam fit the mold of the other Israel executives I had interviewed: He is in his forties and fit. He put his calls on hold and handed me a colorful tile to use as a coaster for my coffee cup. "I bought this years ago at an Arab market. Beautiful, isn't it?"

Q: Could you go to that same market today?

Friedman: I'm not sure.

Q: How much of a challenge has it been to hook up investors with opportunities in Israel?

Friedman: The whole psyche of investors vis-à-vis Israel has changed over the last three and a half years. It's seismic. After a highly publicized terrorist incident, some investors say, "Let's sell. Why do I need this company if I can buy one in America?"

Q: And yet these attacks don't threaten delivery, or do they?

Friedman: It's all a matter of perception. If the investor is uncomfortable, he may look elsewhere. And, in some cases, the unrest may give him the excuse to invest elsewhere. The problem with Israel is that the political and the economic merge so that people are saying, "I won't invest in that economy right now because of the instability, and I won't invest in Israel because of their policies."

Q: And do investors actually say that they wouldn't invest because of Israel's policies?

Friedman: No, but investing is a very personal thing, even with institutions. At the end of the day, there is a portfolio manager making a decision, and if he has a strong political bias, he can easily clothe it with an economic case. It happens much more so now, since the intifada.

But there are long-term concerns that investors and customers have expressed over the last few years—concerns that never came up before. Some are worried about having a single-source provider in Israel, because what if something happens? Others wonder out loud, "What is this crisis doing to the brain drain in Israel?" After all, do you want to invest in a business community when the best talent is fleeing the company and the country? This, by the way, is not happening. There is no brain drain.

And some are concerned about the Israeli government—not that it will fall or anything like that, but will it have the money it used to have? Will the government continue to support future technology with seed companies when they have to spend so much more now on antiterror? For decades, the Israeli government funded a whole slew of incubator companies.

Q: How do you answer their concerns?

Friedman: Well, there are a couple of strategies that may ease the mind of the investor, such as moving manufacturing capability offshore, as a backup, and doing the same with R&D and technology development—moving that to Silicon Valley, for example.

Probably our best response is to put our Israeli CEOs on the road. We literally call it a road show. Many investors are afraid to travel to Israel, so we bring the executives to them—New York, San Francisco, Boston, wherever. This way, our investors can get a personal perspective they cannot get from a news report.

There is a tragic irony in this. We represented, during 9/11, the second-largest venture capital fund in Israel. Since most of [the fund's] money came from American sources, we had a major conference scheduled in New York, because the investors considered Israel an unsafe travel destination. Our conference was scheduled on 9/11! After the planes hit, we were all in shock. A couple of the Israeli managers said to me, "This happens in Israel all the time, but *here* we expected to be safe."

Q: I spoke with one Israeli executive who was on a business trip in Tokyo—and glad to be, at least for a few days, in a country without a decades-long terror problem. As luck would have it, he was on the subway that was attacked with nerve gas. He wasn't hurt, but he said the same thing to me, that he expected to be safe in Tokyo. Are most of the companies you represent high tech?

Friedman: Yes, and there's a good reason for that. There are more Israeli companies listed on the NASDAQ than from any other country. But there are challenges. First, the high-tech bubble burst in the year 2000, then the intifada began. So it was a double hit, and the venture capital started to dry up.

Q: Are a lot of your CEOs and managers, then, former military?

Friedman: Yes, and that's where they learn their trade. Spending three years in the Israeli military means spending three years in one of the most technology-advanced organizations on earth. Those coming out of the military are technological jockeys. Many of these guys continue the relationships forged in the military, and they start up companies. Military experience is pervasive in all Israeli companies; that's why they have a certain can-do attitude. It affects every way in which the company functions, and it affects it positively.

Q: How has life in Israel changed since the intifada?

Friedman: Well, people are checking in with each other all the time, making sure everyone is okay. You check in when you're leaving, and you call when you get there. Everybody does this. And then, when something bad happens, millions of cells phones are ringing. Everybody gets on the phone to say, "I'm okay, Mom."

But, in some ways, life hasn't changed, because we won't let it change. If you look at the cultural events listed in *Time Out*, it's like a phone book. Even in this crisis, the theaters and concert houses are full. It's like New York.

Q: Have you seen businesses trying to help the political situation?

Friedman: Yes, a Jewish friend, in the aluminum business, is doing something very noble, and I think very helpful to the peace process. He has a global business, which means he has friends everywhere, including many Arabs. He has started a project, which involves Palestinians, Egyptians, French, Brits, and Americans, to create a fund to do microlending in the West Bank, to help Palestinians set up a business.

And there are other ways businesses can help. They can support private schools. There is a kindergarten in Jerusalem, for example, where both Arab and Israeli children go to school together. The kids, of course, are too young to know anything about the situation, so they play with each other, as children should. And those friendships hopefully will endure and help the prospects of peace. But maybe it's the parents who benefit even more. Israeli and Arab parents meet each other while picking up the kids, and they have tea, and they talk. Talking is so important.

▪ ▪ ▪

FOCUSING ON THE NEXT GENERATION

As we have seen, some Israeli companies are fighting terror by using methods that one would expect of a business. Terrorists, or their surrogates, have been confronted in the courtroom. Likewise, there are efforts to improve the conditions that contribute to terrorism, such as mass unemployment. Adam Friedman's description of the school, where children and parents of both cultures are brought together, suggests yet another way the Israeli business community can further the cause of peace. Corporate charitable contributions have gone up during the economic recession, not down. While many donations rightly go to helping Israeli victims of terror, the business community wisely puts its resources behind organizations that reach out to the next generation of Palestinians and Israelis.

There are Israeli schools and programs, for example, that are trying to reach across the barriers of hatred and mistrust. One program in particular has made progress in bridging the gap between Palestinian and Israeli youth. Founded in 1993 by author John Wallach, Seeds of Peace has hosted hundreds of teenagers from both cultures in a summer camp atmosphere in the state of Maine. The kids, between thirteen to fifteen years old, live together for one month. While there are workshops facilitated by Arab and Israeli adults, there is also ample time for play and for being a teenager. The children get to know one another under conditions that would be difficult to duplicate in the Middle East. I happened to see a graduation ceremony from one summer camp on cable television. As I recall, perhaps a hundred young people lined up before a stage, awaiting their chance at the microphone. One by one, they stood before the audience—an act of courage in itself for the average teenager—and spoke for a few minutes of what the camp had meant to them. They spoke of the friendships they had made in the most moving terms of affection, humor, and appreciation. Nearly all pledged to find a way to continue the relationships upon returning to their homelands. The Israeli and Palestinian children laughed, wept, and, in some cases, offered prayers for peace. There wasn't a dry eye in the audience, nor in my living room.

To the degree to which businesses support such programs, they are fighting terrorism in a most penetrating way. Not one of those kids returned home harboring stereotypes of the other; not one of them will be susceptible to the momentum of the intifada. Hopefully, the leaders of the future will be graduates of this or similar programs—made possible, in part, by the business community.

FIGHTING THE NEWS MEDIA

The necessity for Adam Friedman's "road show" of Israeli executives is obvious: Investors will not come to Israel, so the executives must go to the investors. But the underlying need to go abroad is to counter the news media. Israeli executives travel in order to convince investors that the grim news images of a country under siege are incorrect. The media can cause more damage to the economy than a suicide bomber—not because it reports the bombing, but because it reports nothing else. Largely because of media reports—true enough, as far as they go—an impression has been created that Israel is a dangerous place to live and to visit. In fact, visitors are in no more danger in Israel than in any civilized country. Indeed, they are much safer, due to the vigilance of law enforcement and the local citizenry. Watchful eyes tend to make the petty criminal go elsewhere. Commonplace crimes against tourists, such as purse snatching, hotel robberies, and muggings, are rare. And while foreigners should exercise discretion in every country, visitors to Israel can take comfort in the fact that violent crime is, statistically, almost nonexistent. More tourists have been killed in transportation accidents in France or Spain or Italy than have been killed in Israel from all causes. The actual tourists are fine; it's the *tourist industry* that has been severely wounded.

We have already seen how Israeli executives counter news images by making personal phone calls following a well-publicized terror attack, and by sharing contingency plans. Press releases, customer newsletters, and most importantly, good NYSE and NASDAQ standings all increase the comfort level of those who do business with Israeli companies. The challenge of countering the media is not insurmountable. While the news is broadcast to everybody, Israeli businesspeople—in industries other than the tourist industry—have only to reach a comparatively small number of customers/investors. Even the hotels, having given up on mass advertising, now profitably focus on smaller, niche groups that continue to visit the country. So the effects of the seeming all-powerful news media are being offset by proactive Israeli business executives where it counts—with the existing customer base. World opinion, however, is another matter.

Without exception, the Israeli business leaders I interviewed thought world opinion regarding Israel was not only out of their hands, but beyond the power of the CEO to influence. Such matters, it seemed, were relegated to the political figures. And while a businessperson might be able to reduce local tensions by increasing the standard of living for potential malcontents, the making of the moral case appeared not to be responsibility of the executives I met. Certainly, making the moral case for Israel is beyond the scope of this book, but it is *not* beyond the responsibilities of the business professional. There are potential customers who will not do business with an Israeli company because they believe Israel is on the wrong side of the issues. To the degree to which that conclusion is based on the situation *as reported by the news media,* the Israeli business community must respond, at every possible public forum.

No matter where an Israeli executive stands with regard to the political situation—and there are plenty on both sides of the issue—all must surely be repulsed by the spectacle of hooded terrorists being "interviewed" by the media and, in many cases, accorded the status of statesmen. *They* are making a moral case, using ringing slogans that resonate with the newsperson's sense of fair play. Those sentiments are broadcast to the world, with the result that bankers, investors, and entrepreneurs in Europe, Asia, and America may refrain from supporting an Israeli company because of what they hear on the evening news. Why wouldn't the Israeli executive be entitled—in fact, obligated—to make the moral case as well? The Israeli executive should take advantage of this forum, and other podiums, to make the *moral* case to the world. When appropriate, the business case should follow. Both arguments may fly in the face of public perceptions, but countering the news media is one of the many challenges faced by the modern CEO in this age of terror.

BIRTHRIGHT ISRAEL

It is noteworthy that Birthright Israel, a program referred to in the interview with Chen Michaeli (see Chapter 1), was begun by two Israeli businessmen. They established a fund to sponsor and subsidize visits for virtually any Jewish eighteen-year-old who has never been to Israel. The program is ingenious. It draws on citizens of other countries to help create moral support for the nation while cultivating in these newest visitors a desire to return—next time on their own dime. The offer is seductive—what young person would turn down a free ten-day "vacation" to Israel? It is also unapologetically selective; Birthright Israel is reserved for the next generation to take its place in the world. Although the Israeli government wisely contributes substantially to the fund, it was not its idea. The business community spawned this program in response to the intifada, in part to usher in guests, with money to spend, for the struggling hotels. Yet the potential impact of the program may be far reaching. Thousands of young people have come and gone, taking an impression with them that will spread, by word of mouth, upon their return home. These positive messages may encourage future tourism and perhaps even immigration. They also contribute to the moral support Israel could use at this time of crisis.

CHAPTER FIVE

Checklist for Managing a Business Under Fire

- ❑ Never underestimate the value of suing the terrorists.
- ❑ Remember, "business" is a universal language.
- ❑ Set the mood for business.
- ❑ Get businesses involved in finding ways to create less fertile conditions for terrorism.
- ❑ Focus on the next generation.
- ❑ Counter the news media, if necessary, to the best of your ability.

CONCLUSION

Preparing for the Long Haul

■ ■ ■

"We don't even refer to it as a 'crisis' anymore; it is normal life for us now."

—JANOS DAMON, DIRECTOR,
ISRAELI HOTEL MANAGERS ASSOCIATION

WHEN A STATE OF "CRISIS" IS PROLONGED OVER A PERIOD OF years, the use of the term becomes less and less appropriate; so many personal and professional adjustments have been made that the conditions that once represented an "emergency" have been thoroughly incorporated into one's way of life. The crisis hasn't passed—it has been absorbed. Those living through this period must think hard to recall life being any different. The intifada, which began in October 2000, may not have reached that stage of complete subconscious acceptance by the Israeli populace, but surely it is close. If Israelis were once surprised by the appearance of metal detectors and guards at virtually every commercial establishment, they would now be surprised by any suggestion that such precautions may one day be unnecessary. Polls indicate that Israeli citizens, while hoping for a dependable condition of peace, have few illusions about the intentions of the terrorists. Most expect the terror to continue, perhaps for years to come.

This rather bleak outlook is, ironically, quite necessary to the mental health of a nation that cannot allow dashed hopes of peace to affect economic prosperity. But it does represent a profound set of challenges to the Israeli business community. Managers can expect, if they have not already witnessed, a change in the people they supervise. The smiles may be less frequent, despite the best efforts of management to cheer up the workplace. And employees may be less inclined to plan for a career with the company, opting instead to think more like free agents, getting what they can out of this or that organization while it is still possible. This situation makes it more difficult for the manager to foster a long-term corporate vision for employees and investors alike.

Managerial leadership skills will be more important during the long haul than during the "emergency," because one can no longer hold the opinion that the terrorist crisis is a temporary condition. While, hopefully, it will not rank up there with the Hundred Years War between France and England, the intifada could last for a good chunk of your business career. Considering the role optimism plays in any economy, a general perception on the part of the local and global business communities that conditions in Israel will not improve for some time can further discourage the investments necessary for an economic revival. The slightest rumor in the American marketplace, for example, can send the comparatively unmolested stock market into a sell-off. What rumors could emanate from an economy that has been under violent assault for years?

Let's examine some of the challenges inherent in preparing the workforce for the long haul.

▪ ▪ ▪

Interview with Dov Lautman,
Chairman of the Board, Delta Galil Industries Ltd.

"You have to show the customer that business will be 'as usual' without *him coming."*

Clothing manufacturer Delta Galil Industries Ltd. makes underwear—nearly $600 million worth of underwear, sold under brands such as Calvin Klein, Hugo Boss, Nike, Ralph Lauren, and Donna Karan. You can buy Delta's products, without even knowing it, through retailers such as Marks & Spencer, Target, Wal-Mart, Victoria's Secret, JCPenney, and The Gap. Headquartered in Israel, Delta operates manufacturing facilities in Israel, Jordan, Egypt, Turkey, Eastern Europe, North and Central America, the Caribbean, and the Far East. It's one of the biggest and oldest companies in Israel. I sat across an enormous desk from Dov Lautman, chairman of the board, who was working on the weekend in a short-sleeved shirt, alone on a floor of suites devoted to the worldwide operations of the company. Since there was no one around to offer amenities, he darted back and forth to the break room to bring me a cup of, as he put it, "good Israeli coffee." Dov gives the impression of having been a physically powerful man in his younger days. He's still a big guy, but relaxed, in his sixties. I was beginning to wonder at this point if there was something in the water responsible for so many senior Israeli executives having all their hair—and, if there was, could I take some home?

Lautman: So you want to learn how we are living underwater?

Q: I beg your pardon?

Lautman: I will tell you. One day God called all the leaders of the world into Heaven. He told them they had made a mess of the world, and that it was time to start the whole experiment over. "Go to your peoples," He thundered, "and tell them in six months I shall cover the earth with another flood." Contrite, the American president advised his countrymen to repent and prepare to meet their Maker. The Russian president told his subjects to eat, drink, and be merry, for soon the world will end. The Israeli prime minister told the Knesset, "We have six months to learn how to live underwater."

Q: Yes, that's exactly why I'm here—to learn how you are living underwater. Let's begin with your market. What portion of Delta's sales is domestic?

Lautman: Not much; ninety-five percent of our sales are in Europe and the United States.

Q: Does that mean your company has not been affected by the intifada?

Lautman: Every company has been affected, to some degree, because of the investment dollars drying up. The natural reaction during a crisis is to "wait and see." In the previous wars, investors and customers waited for a month or so and then saw things return to normal. When the current situation began, in October 2000, investors and customers decided once again to wait and see. But it's been nearly four years! Many investors have tired of waiting and have looked elsewhere [for places] to put their money.

The other side of that coin is our customers also want to wait and see before they visit. We used to have three or four teams from our customers come to us on a weekly basis—to work with us, and to meet with our designers. That has stopped completely. So our managers and our designers have to go there.

Q: You don't try to persuade your customers that it's safe to come to Israel?

Lautman: You can't press the issue too much. You have to show the customer that business will be "as usual" *without* him coming.

By the way, the same applies to our managers abroad. Once the U.S. State Department announced that traveling to Israel is dangerous, it's difficult to tell your manager in New York to come to a meeting in Tel Aviv.

So, as you see, we have a global customer base, but we're still affected by the intifada. The length of the crisis equals a lack of investment, which in turn equals the inability to plan, because you can't forecast demand. So, you really have to pay close attention to your operations. If you look only at averages, it means one part of your business is subsidizing another less profitable part, and if you don't watch and drill down into the details, you will be in big trouble.

Q: What about your European and American customers—have they expressed concern about your ability to deliver?

Lautman: An American retailer called right before the recent Iraqi War asking, "How can you guarantee shipments to me will not be interrupted?" I told him we have gone through many wars here without a slippage in delivery. But, to calm his fears, I gave him a contingency plan.

Q: When I met with Benny Gaon, he told me about the success of the Erez industrial zone. He said the important thing was to make basic products. Underwear would certainly qualify. Are some of your products made in qualifying industrial zones?

Lautman: Yes, we have a factory in Egypt that employs 12,000, and one in Jordan, with 2,500 workers.

Q: No problems involving politics?

Lautman: [Laughing] We don't put an Israeli flag on the roof, if that's what you mean. But everybody there knows we're an Israeli company. I can tell you honestly that there's never been a problem since we opened the factory twenty-nine years ago. And there are Israelis working there, right alongside the Arabs.

And I just don't mean that there has been no fighting. We've never even had *arguments*, or anti-Israeli graffiti on the bathroom walls.

Q: Are the Israelis the managers?

Lautman: Not necessarily. Workers are promoted to the ranks of management according to their ability, not their nationality. So everyone feels as if they can succeed, because they see their friends rising to management.

This is a very good thing for peace in the region. These Jordanian and Egyptian workers go to their homes at night and hopefully influence their parents and their own children.

Q: Is it difficult, from an administrative point of view, working with the governments of Jordan and Egypt?

Lautman: [Laughing] Sometimes I think we get along better with the governments and the bureaucracies over there than we do here.

Q: If these factories are possible in Jordan and Egypt, have you ever had one in the West Bank?

Lautman: You can't expect businesses to go where areas are not secure. It's really sad, because this company alone could employ thousands of people in the West Bank and further help the cause of peace. But there's no security. Erez is successful, because it's on our border and the IDF [Israel Defense Forces] can provide the security. And frankly, it helps us, too. Part of the win-win of an industrial zone is that it helps secure the border, because it's in the interest of everybody not to have incidents that will close the factories.

Q: Have other businesses from other countries tried to take advantage of the lower labor costs in Jordan and Egypt and opened up their own factories?

Lautman: No, because you have to know how to work in different cultures. It's very hard for a Japanese or an American company to set up shop in the Middle East and not make mistakes—you know, cultural gaffs. This region is very unique, and we are part of it.

If we could join forces, this region could be very competitive. Why should the Europeans buy from China when they could buy from here—Egypt, Jordan, and Israel? We are three days to Europe by boat, while China is three weeks by boat. Most retailers value *time* even more than the 5 percent they might save on the cost.

Q: Are you optimistic for that kind of harmony to take place?

Lautman: Yes, we are at peace with Jordan and Egypt. As to the rest of it, I'm not sure. Sometimes the peace process can be better for investment than peace itself, because companies want to get in, ahead of the actual peace, before all of their competitors will come. What we need, though, is a light at the end of the tunnel for all these companies to see.

Not knowing when it will end makes it very difficult. If we knew, for example, that we have to endure a poor economy for a year, then we could say okay and plan accordingly. But when you *don't* know, and when it goes on year after year, it becomes a constant corrosion.

Studies have shown that one common characteristic of top businesspeople is optimism. It's hard to be optimistic when you can't see the light at the end of the tunnel.

Q: What did you do in the military?

Lautman: I was a captain in the Engineer Corps. I was in the Sinai War in 1956, then in the Six Day War in 1967.

Q: Does your military training help you lead Delta through this crisis?

Lautman: Sure, and it helps my younger managers. They are very mature. When I went to MIT, I had already spent three years in the army. To me, the other kids seemed like children.

But I wish there wasn't the need for compulsory service. When an Israeli child is born, we give a toast: "Please God that he won't have to go into the army." I said that over my children, but they went into the army. I say it now over my grandchildren; I hope it won't be necessary for them to go.

It used to be Jewish mothers wanted their sons to be doctors; today, they want them to become software engineers–but not soldiers. The dream for our children is prosperity, education, not military service.

▪ ▪ ▪

REPLACING OPTIMISM WITH DETERMINATION

A lack of optimism does not necessarily translate into poor economic performance. In fact, it can be argued that Israeli companies are rock solid because of their indifference to rumors of peace or war. When hope is gone, despair is not the only alternative—impassivity can take its place. The Israeli CEOs, executives, and managers I interviewed all had an implacable air about them, behind the charm, behind the humor. Like soldiers too long in battle—or like patients whose constant pain has finally smoothed the facial features—these managers were imperturbable. I had the impression they would neither jump for joy at the signing of a peace treaty, nor fall into despair at its first violation; they were in a zone all their own. Although affected to various degrees by world opinion, they seemed unconcerned, and nearly dismissive. This was *their* country, *their* economy, *their* responsibility, and they seemed utterly capable of leading their organizations to even higher levels of performance.

The question, of course, is, "How long can someone maintain a high level of performance without hope of things getting better?" And I think the answer is: "Longer than one can exist on hope alone." The Israeli business community has demonstrated to the world that the issue of peace with terrorists *as a prerequisite for business excellence* should be forgotten. Peace is not a realistic possibility as long as there are legions of fanatics in the world, and it should be completely irrelevant to the profitable functioning of a business. If there is cause for optimism, it is the certainty that the civilized societies will eventually reduce the frequency of terrorist attacks to an acceptable level. Just as organized crime has been controlled but not conquered, terrorism can be stifled. In the meantime, optimism itself should not be considered a necessary attribute for business success. Far more important is the kind of single-minded dedication to excellence, as exhibited by Israeli executives and managers, despite—and in spite of—the terror.

Interview with Ziv, Barbara, and Shai, Israel's Future Business Leaders

"I see the next generations, on both sides, growing up hating each other."

After conducting more than thirty interviews, my stay in Israel was coming to an end. On my last night, around ten o'clock, I had the chance to sit with some of the friends I had made in or about the hotel. I wanted to round out the interview schedule—which included so many CEOs and senior executives—with three young people who were not reflecting on a long career, but looking ahead to one. We sat in the lobby of the David Intercontinental, off in a quiet corner, drinking tea. Each of us had already put in a long day, and the general sense of fatigue was, in itself, an interview aid. The conversation seemed to cut to the heart of the issues without meandering. Ziv is perhaps twenty-eight years old; she manages a bar frequented by tourists and local businesspeople. Attractive and friendly, she seems a natural hostess. Barbara is a business development manager, twenty-seven years old, slightly reserved, and also quite attractive. Whereas Ziv's hair is down, Barbara's is in a tight bun. With her stylish glasses, she reminded me of a pretty librarian I had fallen hopelessly in love with as a child. Shai (pronounced "Shay") is barely thirty and an accountant. He is a veteran of the Israeli "Cherry Unit." Something may be lost in the translation, because the Cherry Unit is the IDF's elite urban fighting division, which is equivalent to the U.S. Army Green Berets or the British SAS. Still waters run deep, because Shai is the mildest person you'll ever meet.

Q: We're sitting across from the Dolphinarium. How do each of you remember that night?

Ziv: [Looking out the window toward the darkened building] I had just finished the early shift and got home about nine that night. Suddenly, my phone started ringing off the hook. All my friends were suddenly calling; they knew I worked near the Dolphinarium. That's how I found out there had been a bombing.

Coming to work the next day, the hotel was almost empty. It seemed like all the tourists had left.

Even if they had had a security guard that night, it wouldn't have done any good. The bomber mingled in the long line, waiting to get to the security guard at the door. When he felt himself surrounded by the most people, he blew himself, and them, up.

Barbara: I heard the explosion. Minutes later, my girlfriend called and told me her brother was at the Dolphinarium and was helping with the wounded.

Since I've been here, I've been close to—close enough to hear—three bombings: the Dolphinarium, Dizengoff Center, and Café Bialik. Still, this is my home and I will never leave.

Shai: It was the first bombing in a dance club that I remember. The Dolphinarium was a favorite hangout by Russian immigrants to Israel. Twenty-eight were killed. They were just children; the average age was sixteen.

Since then, something changed for me privately, and I think it changed for the government and society as well. I was very angry.

Q: By the way, did any of you immigrate to Israel?

Barbara: I came here from Belgium ten years ago.

Q: After being close to three bombings, did you ever second-guess your decision to move to Israel?

Barbara: Never. I was more afraid in Belgium. There, I can be raped in the street; I can be robbed. Things like that don't happen here; or, if they do, it's very, very rare. I can go home late at night from work and not worry. In Belgium, a woman would never venture out alone; even in daylight, it's dangerous.

Everything is for young people here. It's so different from Europe. Here, in Israel, people give you a chance.

Q: Is it difficult to plan for a career under these circumstances?

Ziv: It's very hard to plan. We keep saying, "Maybe next year it will be okay." Then we say it again the year after.

Barbara: I think it's easier for a man to plan his life in Europe. In Belgium, a man at twenty-two may be a little more focused. He has graduated from the university, and he knows what he wants to do with his life. An Israeli man the same age has been in the army instead, and then goes off to India—99 percent of the former soldiers take a year off. So, when he returns to Israel, he may not be sure of what he wants to do with his life.

Q: Was that the case with you, Shai?

Shai: I did not stay long in India. I wanted to come back and get to work.

Ziv: After the army, and *because of the army*, they need to go away, to feel free. All this talk about how the army makes a man of you. . . . They're not soldiers; they're children. Who wants to be in the army? Nobody. But we've got to go.

Shai: [Grinning] Ziv was one of my instructors in boot camp.

Ziv: [Exhaling cigarette smoke] I was his physical fitness instructor. Actually, it was easier for me. All the men had to run with their heavy gear on, while the instructors could wear shorts.

Q: You're all intelligent, ambitious people. What's it like living here, during this crisis?

Barbara: When you get on a bus, everybody looks at everybody else. I make a point of opening my coat casually, so they can see I have no explosives on a belt. I look around, too.

Ziv: I'll give you an example. I went to a mall in Barcelona a few months ago. Nobody checked my bag. I opened it automatically as I went through the door, but there was no one to check it. It felt wonderful just to walk inside a mall without worry.

Shai: I'm working on two projects where terrorism is an issue. One is a project for El Al [Israel Airlines]. They were hit hard, not only by terror here in Israel, but abroad. The number of passengers dropped dramatically while the costs of security went way up.

The second project is the Jerusalem light rail train, now being built. The government, by contract, has to protect the investor from terrorist events—by way of compensation, if one should happen, and by security systems to prevent one from happening. Otherwise, no investor would have put up money.

Q: I guess what I mean is, how do you handle the violence emotionally?

Barbara: It's strange. After three and a half years, we are not surprised by the bombings. So when they happen, we don't ask, "Why?" the way a person might in another country. We are not shocked by a suicide bombing.

Ziv: And it's not always a suicide bomber. They left a time bomb in the cafeteria at the University of Jerusalem. A number of students were killed as they were eating lunch. That's why every bag left unattended is such a concern. We all back away and call the police. It happens every day.

Shai: The bomber is not always male. At the Maxim restaurant in Haifa, it was a female. She ate a complete meal, *paid* for it, and then, surrounded by families of customers, blew herself up. Twenty-one were killed. In the case of one family, three generations were murdered—grandfather, mother, child.

Q: Do any of you see a light at the end of the tunnel?

Ziv: As long as five-year-olds are taught in schools that Jews drink the blood of Arab babies, do *you* see a solution? I see the next generations, on both sides, growing up hating each other.

Shai: When they talk about hate, it's always in the context of the terrorists hating us. But our young children are exposed to terror; many of them have lost sisters and fathers to terrorists, while their brothers are killed in the army. They learn to hate, too.

▪ ▪ ▪

THE ACCEPTANCE OF HATRED

It is doubtful that many business schools cover the subject of "dealing with hatred," but the issue is of great relevance in the age of terror, when business communities are confronted with boycotts, at a minimum, and terrorist attacks, in the worst case. Since businesses are made up of people, after all, it is wise to acknowledge the very human reaction to suddenly becoming an object of hatred. Most of us are uncomfortable when we discover somebody wishes us ill; in fact, we feel wronged. Certain that there has been a misunderstanding, we earnestly set about trying to make amends; we won't feel good again until psychological peace is restored. Later, as we realize we are being hated for values that we will not forsake, the soul begins to stiffen. The acceptance of being the target of hatred represents a profound psychological adjustment and an irrevocable loss of innocence.

Israelis have accepted the hatred; they do not wring their hands, wondering why. Once this unfortunate fact of life is confronted and accepted, the fear of the terrorist seems almost to dissipate. Once an enemy is acknowledged, he is no longer in the shadowy periphery of one's consciousness; he is illuminated by one's steady awareness, and, oddly, he becomes much less frightening in appearance. Israeli businessmen and women have no problem recognizing that there are many in the world who would literally kill them, and their families, without a second thought, if only given the opportunity. That kind of shocking discovery represents a coming-of-age early in the development of the Israeli character, though it must be a pity for any father and mother to witness. No parent wants to search for the words to explain why a child is the target of what amounts to a genocidal hatred.

Israeli children who trot off to school carrying a gas mask will one day work in, or manage, a business. They will have a significant psychological advantage over contemporaries abroad. While the acceptance of hatred is difficult enough for an individual, for a business it is positively traumatic. Businesses want to be loved, by as many segments of the marketplace as possible; hence the reluctance on the part of businesses to be associated with any political stance. CEOs do not want to alienate any potential customer group, so they avoid controversy at all costs. As few as ten or twenty complaint letters make the boldest business leaders blanch, because they know that for every customer who takes the time to write, scores of others feel similarly. This is why businesses go to such great lengths to please the customer. The prospect of being positively *hated* by millions of potential customers weakens the knees of many CEOs. Israeli business leaders do not like to lose potential revenue, either. However, they know the change of attitude will have to come from within the lost customer group—not as a result of altering their own business practices.

Many Americans, for the first time in their lives, are facing a fact of life that even the World War II generation did not have to grapple with. Knowing that somebody out there despises you and, furthermore, that there is nothing you can or should do to dissuade the "hater" creates a certain adult state of mind. Regrettably, some endearing American qualities, such as giving the benefit of the doubt to a stranger, have, by necessity, been replaced with caution. Americans do not like being hated, but they seem to have adjusted to the phenomenon by drawing closer to national values.

THE LONG HAUL

At the time of this writing, the Israeli economy has been under assault from this most recent intifada for nearly four years. There is every indication this crisis will continue unabated. While other nations all over the world have also been attacked and are on high alert, Israel is still, by far, the country most harassed by terrorism in the world today. The country's economy has suffered accordingly, but businesses have also become stronger—in terms of operational efficiency and in positioning for the future. The hard lessons learned by Israeli executives and managers have been institutionalized into the business culture, which means companies are making money under conditions previously thought to have spelled bankruptcy. That is what makes Israeli best business practices so relevant for the business community worldwide. If Israeli companies are turning a profit *now,* under dire circumstances, the management principles that have emerged from the crucible of the intifada should prove to be even more successful for companies competing under happier economic circumstances. Israeli best practices work well, whether or not there is a terrorist crisis—and they will remain embedded in its business culture long after the passing of the intifada.

The experience of the Israeli business community with terrorism is also relevant because the war against Israel is obviously also a war against capitalism itself, just as the attack on 9/11 targeted not only *working* New Yorkers but the very symbols of American dominance in the global market: the Twin Towers of the World Trade Center. While innocent human beings are the literal victims, the true target of terrorism is a nation's economy. Terrorists have no armies to field, nor can they effectively threaten military formations with defeat. They feel they *can*, however, go to the heart of the opposition by attacking the comparatively unguarded economy. Damage to an economy can be inflicted at grotesquely disproportionate costs. For the price of fifteen box cutters, terrorists wreaked havoc in New York that only historians will be able to accurately measure. Economies are absurdly vulnerable to attack, from all sides and from oblique angles. True, free enterprise systems are protected by armed forces ready to, if need be, enforce the rules of the game. But within the perimeter of the guarded playing field, even a robust economy is vulnerable precisely because it presents so many "soft" targets. In the hopes of toppling a government from within or, at the very least, forcing concessions upon a beleaguered public, terrorists will try to make life miserable for their opponents by destroying the means to enjoy life.

Anyone with the slightest business experience would acknowledge that running a successful operation under the most benign conditions is a difficult enough proposition. For all of its virtues, the free enterprise system is fraught with risk. Businesses open and fail every day, in a perpetual cycle of birth and death. Success is often characterized by critics of capitalism as a "dog eat dog" world. But even the boldest executives would reel at the prospect of operating a business where fanatics are trying to *murder* their customers, destroy investor confidence, and spread fear throughout the society at large. Israeli executives and managers have no choice in the matter; they must engage in all the usual struggles of operating a business in an increasingly competitive marketplace while simultaneously dealing with a continuing terrorist campaign.

Even after 9/11, many of us may have difficulty imagining business life under conditions similar to those endured by Israeli companies. The constant terror alerts that affect commuter traffic, the gas mask in the desk, the emergency drills at the workplace—all would strike us as very sobering working conditions, indeed. Yet, over time, we might grow accustomed to these conditions, as the Israelis have, and occupy ourselves with traditional business challenges. The executives, managers, and team leaders interviewed herein have dealt with anxieties their counterparts in America—and elsewhere in the world of free enterprise—are just now beginning to face. Just as the police and military from many nations now travel to Israel to study under the tutelage of the security "experts," so too can business leaders from all nations learn from those who, sadly, have had to become expert in the art of business management under the relentless threat of terrorism.

Concluding Checklist for Managing a Business Under Fire

- ❑ Replace optimism with determination and impassivity.
- ❑ Accept the "fact of life" of hatred.
- ❑ Prepare for the long haul.

Index

■ ■ ■